THE DECLINE OF HUMILITY AND THE DEATH OF WISDOM

THE DECLINE OF HUMILITY AND THE DEATH OF WISDOM

The Source of Modern Society's
Problems and the Key to the Solutions

WILLIAM TULLY

The Decline of Humility and the Death of Wisdom.
Copyright © 2020 by William Tully. All rights reserved.

No part of this publication may be reproduced, stored in a retrieval system or transmitted in any way by any means, electronic, mechanical, photocopy, recording or otherwise without the prior permission of the author except as provided by USA copyright law.

Book design copyright © 2020. Raket Creatives.
Project Manager and Team Coordinator Mary Cindell Lynn Pilapil
Cover design by Jim Villaflores
Interior design by Vanz Edmar Mariano

Published in the United States of America

Hardback: 978-1-7357460-0-5
Paperback: 978-1-7357460-1-2
Ebook: 978-1-7357460-2-9

Non-Fiction/ Philosophy/World History
October 07, 2020

DEDICATION

I dedicate this book to my loving wife, Lori, and our three daughters, Erin, Allison and Christine. They have been my constant inspiration as they have successfully kept me humble and provided ample opportunities to practice patience and understanding.

I would also like to acknowledge Nancy Stokes for her invaluable editing insight, and for all my family and friends (as well as foes) for their continual lessons in humility.

PREFACE

In 1971, I was a freshman starting high school, and encountered my first example of what I recognized as true wisdom. As those of my generation will remember, we had a major technological breakthrough with the Xerox photostatic copy machines. Before the age of cell phone and Multi-purpose Internet Mail Extensions (MIMES). People would simply photocopy interesting documents or cartoons, jokes, etc., and pass them onto friends. As the item was copied multiple times, the copies would become increasingly dark and have a lot of black marks which made it increasingly difficult to read.

That first piece of recognized wisdom was entitled "Desiderata," (loosely translated from Latin as "that which is desired") and it was dark and difficult to read. It was attributed as "Anonymous" and was supposedly found on a wall of an old abandoned country church. The mystery of its origin made its words all the more impactful. I committed the opening and closing stanzas to memory:

> "Go placidly amid the noise and haste and remember what peace there may be in silence."

"As far as possible without surrender be on good terms with all persons. Speak your truth quietly and clearly and listen to others, even the dull and ignorant: they too have their story."

"With all its sham, drudgery, and broken dreams, it is still a beautiful world. Be cheerful. Strive to be happy."

As I began to write this book, I tried to find a copy of Desiderata – obviously I had no idea as to what may have become of my old Xerox copy. To my surprise, the internet not only provided a copy of the document, but it also provided an author, Max Ehrmann (1927). I guess it wasn't really a mysterious, anonymous work afterall. However, it is still an excellent example of wisdom. A full copy of Desiderata is available on the Internet, as well as in the book <u>The Poems of Max Ehrmann</u>, published by his widow, Bertha K. Erhmann, and I would strongly encourage everyone to read it. After all:

"You are a child of the universe, no less than the trees and the stars; you have a right to be here.

And whether or not it is clear to you, no doubt the universe is unfolding as it should."

From Desiderata

INTRODUCTION

    Every generation is tempted to question the "signs of the times," worry about the "new generation," and wonder whether we are facing the end of the world as we know it. It is easy for someone with a limited sense of history to simply ignore such concerns. However, a closer examination of history could support a conclusion that we are, indeed, living in very frightening times.

    As of 2020, the world population is estimated to be between 7.5 and 7.8 billion persons. It is also a time when food production, manufacturing, and technological advances are at an all-time high, yet world headlines are full of fears of impending disaster. Despite a record production of food, that food often doesn't make its way to the neediest populations because of inadequate infrastructure and/or corrupt governments.

    We have more information available to us at our fingertips, but we have difficulty understanding it or applying it effectively in our lives. That information is further complicated because the internet and social media are now subject to unprecedented manipulation and corruption of information. Moreover, the state of public discourse is at an all-time low with people yelling at each other instead of conversing civilly. Ironically, despite all of our investments in education at all levels, some have argued that U.S. citizens are individually smarter, but collectively dumber than ever before.

We see the death toll increasingly rising with drug abuse – especially with opioids. Addictions are not limited by age or demographics. Fentanyl is present in such supply and at such a cheap price, it is replacing heroin, and even methamphetamine, for unsuspecting addicts who purchase street drugs. Although many addicts become addicted from legally prescribed pain medications, far more have become addicted through progressive abuse of street drugs. Many are "self-medicating" for anxiety, depression, PTSD, and countless other ailments. Those psychological disorders seem to be diagnosed at record-breaking frequency.

Our society also suffers from chronic rudeness and incivility. Anger is displayed publicly, both in real life and on television. "Aggressive driving" has reached epidemic levels, and incidents of "road rage" clog our criminal dockets. Human trafficking is happening virtually everywhere, including in our own local communities. Little value is placed on human life, or on how we interact with each other personally. The anger and vitriol is ever more apparent in social media.

I am not sure if modern politics is a reflection of our society, or if our society reflects the incivility in the political arena. In any event, U.S. politics has probably never been more divisive, vitriolic, and unhealthy (which is saying a lot considering how nasty early U.S. politics were – such as one of the original political fights which ended in a fatal pistol

THE DECLINE OF HUMILITY AND
THE DEATH OF WISDOM

duel between Aaron Burr and Alexander Hamilton in 1804.) Clearly, there has been a move away from policy debate toward personal name calling and nasty Machiavellian power politics.

Perhaps the most significant symptom of today's world is general anxiety. In addition to the frequency of clinical anxiety, most citizens feel overwhelmed watching the news. There is no shortage of news stories involving civil unrest throughout the planet. There is also the ongoing threat of terrorism – world and domestic. There are threats of world pandemics, wars, economic collapses, and even fears of climate change. There is 24/7 coverage of earthquakes, volcanoes, and tsunamis. Moreover, many people seem to get even more upset with the fact that they can't get everyone else to join their personal crusade to combat any one or more of those world threats.

Anxiety grows, anger increases, frustration abounds, and we no longer communicate with each other civilly. Instead of civilized conversations over coffee or cocktails, which usually led to better understanding, or at least an "agreement to disagree," we combat each other through texts, emails, Facebook posts, Tweets, Instagrams, etc. When we don't communicate face-to-face, and with empathy or compassion, the communications become uncivilized and even caustic.

As we become increasingly atomized, divided, and pessimistic, our leaders don't seem to try and help. Instead, they seem to enjoy the division as they try to score potential political capital. Society no longer seems to acknowledge a higher authority (whether that be God or any higher law such as a Constitution.). Even the "Golden Rule" seems to have vanished from the public square. Where are we to turn for answers?

As a historian by education, a lawyer by trade, and a trial judge by current vocation, I looked hard to identify causes for this societal morass. There certainly are no easy answers, nor any single cause. I eventually concluded that the answer lay in the decline of two independent, yet inter-related values in American society: humility and wisdom. This decline had its origin centuries ago, but it has accelerated rapidly over the last fifty years.

At the time of the American Revolution, the virtues of humility and wisdom were almost universally accepted as essential to civilized society. In fact, they were not only personified in the image of George Washington, they became ingrained in our nation's founding principles. George Washington could have claimed credit for his military wins (which would not have been historically accurate), but instead gave all credit to "Providence." He could have accepted the role of "King," but instead he accepted the office of "President." Through his humility he learned and grew in wisdom, letting that humility and wisdom guide him not only in how he served as our first President, but also in his parting advice to the nation contained in his Farewell Address.

As our society has evolved away from humility toward arrogance, and from wisdom toward conceit, the ills we experience today were probably inevitable. This book is intended to better define these two important virtues and their interdependence. It will then examine how western

THE DECLINE OF HUMILITY AND THE DEATH OF WISDOM

philosophy not only moved away from the virtue of humility but eventually came to vilify it.

Many of today's problems have been amplified by the modern "virtues" of narcissism and self-absorbed arrogance. Hopefully, by recognizing the root of the problem, we can work on restoring a more civilized society by recognizing the benefits of humility: understanding, respect for others, gratitude, kindness, and contentment. The result of living and experiencing these qualities is that good judgment is certain to follow. Collective wisdom is the mechanism to best address the world's current problems and future challenges.

CHAPTER ONE

HUMILITY

"In peace there is nothing so becomes a man as modest stillness and humility."
William Shakespeare

"The best of people is the one who humbles himself the more his rank increases."
Prophet Muhammad

"Do nothing out of selfish ambition or vain conceit. Rather, in humility value others above yourselves."
Philippians 2:3

"If anyone tells you that a certain person speaks ill of you, do not make excuses about what is said of you but answer, 'He was ignorant of my other faults, else he would not have mentioned these alone.'"
Epictetus

"Humility is attentive patience."
Simone Weil

"What the world needs is more geniuses with humility: there are so few of us left."
Oscar Levant

"Think lightly of yourself and deeply of the world."
Miyamoto Musashi

"Humility is the solid foundation of all virtues."
Confucius

"To become truly great, one has to stand with people, not above them."
Charles de Montesquieu

"Humility, that low, sweet root, from which all heavenly virtues shoot."
Thomas Moore

"Humility is the essence of love and intelligence; it is not an achievement."
Jiddu Krishnamurti

"Pride makes us artificial and humility makes us real."
Thomas Merton

"A great man is always willing to be little."
Ralph Waldo Emerson

"Humility must always be the portion of any man who receives acclaim earned in the blood of his followers and the sacrifices of his friends."
Dwight D. Eisenhower

THE DECLINE OF HUMILITY AND
THE DEATH OF WISDOM

"There is no respect for others without humility in one's self."

Henri-Frederic Amiel

"Humility forms the basis of honor, just as the low ground forms the foundation of a high elevation."

Bruce Lee

Everyone probably has an innate understanding of what humility means; however, giving it a definition can be a challenge. According to the Merriam Webster dictionary, humility is described as "the state of being humble." Both it (humility) and humble have their origin in the Latin word "humilis" meaning "lowly". Obviously, the dictionary's use of the word being defined in the actual definition adds little clarity. From the ascribed synonym we get a little better picture: "demureness, down-to-earthiness, humbleness, lowliness, meekness, modesty."

Perhaps we can learn more from looking at its antonyms, or what humility is not: "arrogance, assumption, bumptiousness, conceit, egotism, haughtiness, imperviousness, loftiness, lordiness, pomposity, presumptuousness, pretentiousness, pridefulness, superiority." A better definition of humble might be the absence of arrogance, conceit and egoism.

After viewing humility and its opposite qualities, one would conclude that a person who is genuinely humble would be much more pleasant to be with, than an arrogant, egotistical, pompous fool. If you think about it, when you are around a genuinely humble person, you tend to relax because you know that you are being heard and not judged.

Moreover, when one thinks of a perfect model of humility, the example of Mother Teresa of Calcutta may come to mind. She, herself, described humility as follows:

> "Humility is the mother of all virtues; purity, charity and obedience, it is in being humble that our love becomes real, devoted and ardent. If you are humble, nothing will touch you, neither praise nor disgrace, because you know what you are. If you are blamed, you will not be discouraged. If they call you a saint, you will not put yourself on a pedestal."

Essentially, humility allows us to live a life free of pride, pomposity, and arrogance (or any of the other previously listed antonyms). It is often characterized as having a modest view of oneself and having gratitude and a lack of hubris.

> "There is a thin line between confidence and arrogance…it's called humility. Confidence smiles, arrogance smirks."
>
> Anonymous

Humility allows us to appreciate that we are not on this planet alone, and that the world does not revolve around us. It requires us to view all our fellow human beings as equal in humanity and possessing human dignity. How we treat each other is of paramount importance. Gordon B. Hinkley, an American religious leader and author, (who served as the 15th President of the Church of Jesus Christ of Latter Day Saints) wrote:

THE DECLINE OF HUMILITY AND THE DEATH OF WISDOM

"Being humble means recognizing that we are not on earth to see how important we can become, but to see how much difference we can make in the lives of others."

Arrogance blocks our ability to see the importance of others. Self-centered individuals often see others as people who need to be subjugated to their will. They see no social contract that applies to themselves. They view themselves above everyone else.

Humility improves our ability to interact with others in a civilized manner. That begins by viewing ourselves realistically – seeing our faults and imperfections as clearly as we want to see our gifts:

"True humility is being able to accept criticisms as graciously as we accept compliments."
Sabrina Newby

"Humility isn't denying your strengths; it's being honest about your weaknesses."
Pastor Rick Warren

"Humility is one of the most important qualities which you must have because…if you make people realize that you are no threat to them, then people will embrace you."
Nelson Mandela

> "Humility leads to strength and not to weakness. It is the highest form of self-respect to admit mistakes and to make amends for them."
>
> John J. McCloy

Historically the virtue of humility was almost universally accepted as paramount by all early civilizations. Born approximately in 600 D.C., Lao Tzu was the most respected of all Chinese philosophers. He is accredited with founding Taoism and eventually inspiring the young Confucius. He formed his philosophical teachings allegedly out of disgust for the infamous, cruel, corrupt, and inept politicians of his time.

By tradition it is said that Lao Tzu, at a ripe old age, advised a young Confucius to get rid of his pride, ambitions, and affectation. According to that narrative, Confucius was so impressed by the wise old man, that he dedicated himself to a philosophy which concentrated more on inner-wealth than on outward display. Lao Tzu is accredited with the following quote:

> "I have three precious things which I hold fast and prize. The first is gentleness; the second is frugality; the third is humility, which keeps me from putting myself before others."

Throughout ancient Greek mythology, "hubris" (the opposite of humility) was the downfall of many protagonists. Homer's Iliad, and its sequel, the Odyssey, point out the

THE DECLINE OF HUMILITY AND
THE DEATH OF WISDOM

virtue of humility before the gods, and the resultant harm from the vice of human hubris.

The Greek virtue of humility was exemplified by the character of Socrates (4th century B.C.), who lived in total humility, and was constantly ridiculed by the popular culture of his time. His most famous student, Plato, stated that Socrates never claimed any real knowledge for himself. In fact, Socrates stated that there was a correlation between humility and wisdom:

> "True wisdom comes to each of us when we realize how little we understand about life, ourselves, and the world around us."

In the Old Testament the Angel Lucifer was full of hubris and desired to raise himself above God causing him to be cast down from heaven and into hell. Isaiah 14:11-16. And in Proverbs 3:34 , it is written that "God opposes the proud and gives grace to the humble." The Hindu faith asserts that humility leads to pure knowledge, and Buddhists believe that one cannot attain enlightenment unless he has first perfected humility. Even the word "Islam" means submission to Allah.

A central theme in Christianity is that humility is a virtue and vanity is a sin: "whoever exalts himself will be humbled and whoever humbles himself will be exalted. Matthew 23.12. According to Christian belief, the Lord King (Messiah) Jesus was born in abject poverty lying in a manger and sharing the stable with lowly farm animals. He then lived his life humbly, carrying no possessions, and finally allowed Himself to suffer a horrendous death designed for a common criminal.

Virtually all cultures and faiths have exalted the virtue of humility throughout history. Therefore, one would have to ask why humility is viewed by modern society as a vice or a sign of weakness or failure. Similarly, why does modern society seem to reward hubris, celebrate arrogance, and encourage everyone to have a strong (albeit false) sense of pride? How did we become a "me-first" egocentric culture? How did the ancient vice of narcissism become today's popular virtue? That question will be addressed in a later chapter.

CHAPTER TWO

WISDOM

"Knowing yourself is the beginning of wisdom."
Aristotle

"True wisdom comes to each of us when we realize how little we understand about life, ourselves and the world around us."
Socrates

"Wise men speak because they have something to say; fools because they have to say something."
Plato

"The fool doth think that he is wise, but the wise man knows himself to be a fool."
William Shakespeare

"Knowing others is intelligence; knowing yourself is true wisdom. Mastering others is strength; mastering yourself is true power."
Lao Tzu

"Wisdom is not a product of schooling, but of a lifelong attempt to acquire it."
Albert Einstein

"Honesty is the first chapter in the book of wisdom."
Thomas Jefferson

"By these methods, we may learn wisdom: first by reflection, which is the noblest; second, by imitation which is the easiest; and third by experience, which is the bitterest."
Confucius

"Wisdom is the principal thing. Therefore, get wisdom. And in all your getting, get understanding."
Proverbs 4:7

"Even death is not to be feared by one who has lived wisely."
Buddha

"Turn your wounds into wisdom."
Oprah Winfrey

"Knowledge comes, but wisdom lingers."
Alfred Lord Tennyson

THE DECLINE OF HUMILITY AND THE DEATH OF WISDOM

If we had thought "humility" was a hard term to define, let's try "wisdom." Chances are that we can all recognize it when we see or hear it. We would probably define it as the quality of being "wise," even adding the quality of having experience, knowledge, and good judgment. Surprisingly, Wikipedia might have the most comprehensive definition:

> "The ability to think and act using knowledge, experience, understanding, common sense and insight. Wisdom is associated with attributes such as unbiased judgment, compassion, experienced self-knowledge, self-transcendence and non-attachment, and virtues such as ethics and benevolence."

Wisdom starts with basic intelligence, which in turn allows one to obtain knowledge. Knowledge must then be used to gain fundamental understanding, which is derived through reflection. Life experience provides a critical ingredient: perspective, or the ability to discern where something may fit in to the larger picture. The more experience one has observing how the world works, as well as pondering the lessons of history, leads to a deeper understanding which enhances the ability to exercise good judgment. True wisdom is understanding that this process is a lifelong, never-ending process.

Although wisdom can only be acquired through experience, experience itself does not result in wisdom. There are indeed people who simply are unable to learn from experience. Sometimes a person is able to learn from experience, but can only apply the lesson learned to an identical fact situation. What is the quality that allows one to transfer experience into wisdom? Psychologists have many theories, and researchers are trying to discern which cognitive processes and which social, emotional, and cultural factors might affect one's ability to convert experience into wisdom.

Although it appears that magnitude of experience, as well as depth and diversity of knowledge may be important factors, there is no clear answer. Why are there many well-educated and well-read individuals who cannot reach the threshold of wisdom, when there are much less educated individuals who seem to have an innate "common sense" which can approach wisdom? The answer may lie in the interaction of wisdom and humility. Humble people know that they need to perpetually learn. An arrogant person thinks he knows everything already, or he may believe that he is right, and therefore, never needs to re-evaluate a situation. The next chapter will expand upon this concept.

Why is wisdom worth attaining? It is not essential to survival. Many would contend that society today doesn't even recognize wisdom as a virtue, let alone appreciate its intrinsic value. One could argue that we have more information and knowledge at our disposal today than ever before. Historically, advanced knowledge was only available to a select few through the world's great libraries or institutions of higher learning. Today, formal education is almost guaranteed in the United States. Free primary and secondary public education is not only available but is mandated. Of course, just because formal education is available and mandated doesn't mean that the opportunity to learn is fully accepted or appreciated. Many public-school teachers consistently complain about poor school attendance. Even when students do attend, they

THE DECLINE OF HUMILITY AND THE DEATH OF WISDOM

are often not fully engaged. Being present when knowledge is extended doesn't translate directly to that knowledge being accepted by or incorporated into the student's intellect.

Similarly, today's technology, particularly the internet, provides enormous amounts of information at everyone's fingertips. Not only is that information readily available, it is easily accessible and affordable. Unfortunately, in addition to reliable information, there is also unreliable and incorrect information available as well. If students do not learn to think critically, they will not be able to discern between useful information and dangerous disinformation.

Taking information and translating it into knowledge is only the first step toward wisdom. A more difficult challenge is translating knowledge into understanding. Early elementary education concentrates on memorization and the basic skills of "learning." As any educator will tell you, memorization of facts is not really education. Instead, they are merely the building blocks for learning. Learning to write letters of the alphabet or numerals doesn't translate into knowledge. Rather, they are the basic foundation and necessary tools for obtaining and expressing knowledge.

Being able to access and quote information from the internet is a preliminary step to learning. Even if one were to memorize everything accessed from the internet, it would not translate into understanding. (But if your child was able to accomplish this feat, it would likely earn him or her a spot on Good Morning America as a child prodigy).

As most teachers will tell you, moving from memorization to understanding is a critical step in education. For most, memorization will fade over time; however, understanding will last and provide the basis for future and increased understanding and insight. Therefore, primary education can be considered successful if students reach understanding and the ability to practically apply that understanding in the world around them. That is not "wisdom", but it is clearly an indispensable step in that direction. Higher education builds on primary education in these basic ways: it builds on already accumulated knowledge; it expands upon understanding by dramatically expanding its scope and depth; and it teaches students to think critically. After a successful college education, has a student reached a state of wisdom? Probably not. However, the average college graduate probably has developed a reduced sense of humility because he believes that he has become "educated.".

Growing up, I had the great fortune of spending a substantial amount of time with my maternal grandfather. He was probably the first person I recognized as truly "wise." Despite having his formal education interrupted by World War I, he eventually earned two doctorates and was a Director on the Board of Education of New York City. Although he was extremely well educated, and a career educator, he never considered education to be an end in itself. In fact, he refrained from being addressed as "doctor," and only acknowledged his educational degrees when professionally required to do so.

He was often heard by his family saying "the only degree that matters is an essential degree of intelligence." Similarly, he also stated that "a college degree doesn't mean that you are 'educated,' only that you are educable." My only regret is that I wasn't astute enough at the time to write down more of his

THE DECLINE OF HUMILITY AND
THE DEATH OF WISDOM

quotes. As a child, I must have assumed that he would always be with us. Nevertheless, I do remember him telling me that he learned more important life lessons during World War I than he did in all of his classes. Not only did he fly a SPAD early on in the war, but he trained infantry soldiers in the use and protection from chemical warfare agents. In fact, he lost most of his voice as a result of a training accident when a panicked trainee pulled his gasmask off and exposed him to phosgene gas.

What actually helped my grandfather achieve wisdom? Perhaps it was his experience of the magnitude of a world war which was believed to be the "war to end all wars." Perhaps it was his compensating for the reduction of his voice to a mere hoarse raspy sound. Perhaps it was the great depression followed by a second world war, (which followed the first world war by a mere 21 years). Perhaps it was having to work long days in order to pay for the night classes in pursuit of his education. I can only conclude that it was the humility that he accumulated through all those events, and the practical perspective he gained from all of his dramatic life lessons.

My grandfather rarely dwelled on his accomplishments or attributes, but often listed his shortcoming – especially his loss of patience. At work his nemesis was the proverbial arrogant, political bureaucrat. He often described patience as being similar to a muscle – in that the more you work it, the stronger it became. That phrase always seemed strange coming from a former golden gloves boxer who had an imposing physical build well into his late 70's, yet, he worked his patience the same way he trained his muscles, and his life seemed to continually serve up numerous opportunities to give his patience a workout.

I believe that the most valuable lesson I learned from my grandfather was the clear benefits of wisdom. He always had a sense of balance in life. He was never afraid of the uncertainties of life and faced them all with an eternal sense of optimism. He could always see the bigger picture and accept that there was always enough good in the world to counterbalance all the bad and evil. He always set priorities and dealt with events with a sense of proportion. His loyalty to his faith, family, and society was always placed above his personal desires. He never hesitated to place others before himself, but always knew when to avoid over-extending himself or placing an unfair burden on his wife and two daughters. He nurtured his family and rarely missed an opportunity to educate. He took his greatest pleasure in seeing his daughters, grandchildren, and great-grandchildren grow and prosper.

He was also a person who lived well before his time. He was a pioneer in gender equality and wanted nothing to stand in the way of his daughters' education or vocational ambitions. He also had an advanced knowledge of medicine, anatomy, and kinesiology. I remember him treating our muscle strains with medical tape to provide external support. At the time I would try to hide the tape from my friends thinking that the bandages looked "dorky." Today, over fifty years later, I see professional athletes wearing medical tape to support sprains and strains (and they don't look dorky – they even have designer colors.)

THE DECLINE OF HUMILITY AND
THE DEATH OF WISDOM

His specialty was health education, and he was an instrumental player in President Kennedy's Physical Fitness Award Program. He recognized the need for public education to encourage and promote physical fitness programs. As a child, I thought gym class was stupid during school hours (especially when you could get a lot more innings of baseball played after school than in one hour of school.) But I now see the importance of physical fitness, especially when our nation's youth are worse off today than they were in the 1960's when President Kennedy thought there was a physical fitness crisis. Statistically, the kids in the sixties were less sedentary and less overweight than kids today.

My grandfather's wisdom extended to his view of life in general. Despite his personal and academic accomplishments, he was humbled by his faith. He was extremely prayerful and devoted to passing his faith onto his family. He would often state that his eyesight was saved by a miracle. In his early thirties, he was diagnosed with glaucoma. After extensive treatment by a world renown specialist, he was given twenty-four hours before he would lose his eyesight forever. According to him and my grandmother, instead of losing his eyesight, he was cured within that 24-hour period, to the astonishment of his ophthalmologist. He attributed it to his Novenas to St. Teresa of Avila.

I believe that experience, combined with the aforementioned experiences, gave him a sense of balance in life. Uncertainty did not bring him anxiety, but rather a firm commitment that things would play out well in the end. More importantly, he always saw a balance between himself and others. He was generous to a fault. He respected the earth with all of its inherent balances. And, he had a reservoir of kindness behind his formidable exterior and steel, blue eyes. He is my platinum standard for wisdom. As he would often say, "wisdom is remaining teachable regardless of how much you think that you know." Or, in the words of the 19th Century English preacher:

> "Wisdom is the right use of knowledge. To know is not to be wise, many men know a great deal, and are all the greatest fools for it. There is no fool so great a fool as a knowing fool. But to know how to use knowledge is to have wisdom."
>
> Charles Spurgeon

CHAPTER THREE

CORRELATION BETWEEN HUMILTY AND WISDOM

"The only true wisdom is knowing you know nothing."

Socrates

"Pride leads to disgrace, but with humility comes wisdom."

Proverbs 11:2

"Do you wish to rise? Begin by descending. You plan a tower that will pierce the clouds. Lay first the foundation of humility."

St. Augustine

"Humility is the wisdom of accepting the truth that you might just be wrong."

Richard Paul Evans

"I claim to be a simple individual liable to err like any other fellow mortal. I own, however, that I have humility enough to confess my errors and to retrace my steps."

Gandhi

"Uncertainty is a sign of humility, and humility is just the ability or willingness to learn."

Charles Sheen

"The disadvantages of becoming wise is that you realize how foolish you've been."

Evan Esar

"The greatest lesson in life is to know that even fools are right sometimes."

Winston Churchill

"Humility is the only true wisdom by which we prepare our minds for all the possible changes in life."

George Arliss

"The humble man makes room for progress; the proud man believes he is already there."

Ed Parker

The greatest gift of humility is the recognition of how much we don't know, and the resultant desire and ability to learn. Just as humility is a process of growth (i.e. we never totally reach it), so is wisdom. We never truly reach the status of being wise; however, we are able to perpetually move in that direction. Essentially, humility and wisdom are both evolutions of intellect as individuals mature. Maturity is simply the accumulation of scars from life's difficult, and sometimes painful, lessons.

Wisdom is not merely something that is an end unto itself. Its primary benefit is good judgment. It enables us to make more prudent decisions and better perceive our environment. It places us in a better position to determine where we are in the world as it presently exists, as well as to guide us as to how we should act in furthering a positive impact on that environment. If we are successful, we can ratify our judgment and gain a degree of confidence in it. If we fail, humility allows us to learn from it, and appropriately adapt ourselves and our actions going forward.

Apparently, there is a virtual symbiotic relationship between humility and wisdom. Humility facilitates wisdom; wisdom gained nurtures humility. The wiser we become, and the more we realize the mysteries of the universe, the more humble we become. Just by standing on an ocean shore and gazing upon the vast and seemingly endless horizon, we realize how small and insignificant we truly are. Similarly, viewing the billions of grains of sand within our immediate view, we better realize that each of us is but a single human being among billions who currently inhabit the earth. It is that intellectual humility which leads to open-mindedness, collaboration, and the important sense of being a small part of a much larger entity. We can improve our attitudes toward ourselves and others by living our lives humbly in our relationship with other human beings.

Humble wisdom allows us to constructively converse with one another, and thereby gain knowledge and wisdom from others. As H. Jackson Brown, Jr., stated: "Every person that you meet knows something you don't, learn from them." This can only occur if we respect the value of each and every other human being, or as 16th Century Japanese Philosopher, Miyamoto Musashi once said: "Think lightly of yourself and deeply of the world."

Essentially, although it is true that wisdom can lead to confidence, one must ensure that one's confidence doesn't override humility. We have to avoid any sense that we are in any way superior to our fellow human beings. We may have greater gifts or talents than another person, but that in no way makes anyone superior. Often, one's gifts or talents in one area of life, merely compensate for deficits or unmet needs in other areas of life. In the words of Ernest Hemingway: "There is nothing noble in being superior to your fellow man; true nobility is being superior to your former self." Perhaps, true wisdom is best shown in how we treat each other.

The Old Testament contains the books of wisdom, in one of which, the Book of Proverbs, states:

> "When wisdom comes into your heart, and knowledge is a delight to you, then prudence will be there to watch over you and discernment to be your guardian to keep you away from the way that is evil, from the man whose speech is deceitful, from those who leave the paths of honesty to walk the roads in darkness: men who find their joy in doing wrong, and their delight in deceitfulness…" Proverbs 2:10-15.

THE DECLINE OF HUMILITY AND THE DEATH OF WISDOM

Similarly, in the New Testament's Letter of James the Apostle it states:

> "If there are any wise or learned men among you, let them show it by their good lives, with humility and wisdom in their actions. But if at heart you have the bitterness of jealousy, or a self-seeking ambition, never make any claims for yourself or cover up the truth with lies – principles of this kind are not the wisdom that comes down from above: they are only earthly animals and devilish. Wherever you find jealousy and ambition, you find disharmony, and wicked things of every kind being done: whereas the wisdom that comes down from above is essentially something pure; it also makes for peace, and is kindly and considerate; it is full of compassion and shows itself by doing good; nor is there any trace of partiality or hypocrisy…"
>
> James 3:13-17

There is a clear distinction drawn between wisdom drawn from humility, versus "wisdom" derived through arrogance. The concept of the golden rule is not limited to Judaism and Christianity. It was first documented in early Confucian teaching, and it appears prominently in almost every world religion, including but not limited to Taoism, Islam, Buddhism, and Hinduism. It is also rooted in the essential principles of humanism.

Wisdom, when guided by humility, mandates treating our fellow human beings with respect, equality and perhaps, most importantly, kindness. If this wisdom of the golden rule is almost universally accepted secularly and by most of the world's religions, why is it so hidden in modern society? The answer lies in the evolution (or perhaps devolution) of western society, which started centuries ago. That will be the subject of the next chapter.

CHAPTER FOUR

WESTERN PHILOSOPHY'S MOVE TOWARD ARROGANCE

"Pride makes us artificial and humility makes us real."
Thomas Merton

"It is unwise to be too sure of one's own wisdom. It is helpful to be reminded that the strongest might weaken and the wisest might err."
Gandhi

"Humility is the key to moral excellence. It is the noblest quality a person can possess. It is the mother of all possibilities."
Hsin Yun

"Humility is nothing but truth, and pride is nothing but lying."
Vincent de Paul

> "I speak to everyone the same way, whether he is a garbageman or the President of the United States."
>
> Albert Einstein

> "There is a universal respect and even admiration for those who are humble and even simple by nature, and who have absolute confidence in all human beings irrespective of their social status."
>
> Nelson Mandela

In the early 18th century western philosophy moved in a direction which separated itself from eastern philosophy and the common established tenants of the world's major faiths. It also moved away from the preexisting values and culture of Western Europe.

I do not wish to oversimplify the evolution of western philosophy or ignore the large number of philosophers who contributed to this evolutionary process, but I also do not have the ability to engage in an exhaustive analysis within the parameters of this book. Therefore, I have selected four such philosophers who best exemplify the move toward modern arrogance.

David Hume (1711-1776) was born in Edinburgh, Scotland of noble ancestry, but of limited income. He found his passion in philosophy and acknowledged his love of literary fame. He passionately pursued popular acclaim throughout his life. Although he was classified as an atheist, his thoughts and writings are possibly better classified as anti-organized religion.

Hume concluded that the monotheistic religions of Judaism, Christianity, and Islam were random off-shoots

THE DECLINE OF HUMILITY AND
THE DEATH OF WISDOM

from polytheistic religions and that all religions were simply a way to rationalize peoples' fear of the unknown. Essentially, he believed that religions were simply superstitions designed to explain the unexplainable. Similarly, he concluded that all morality was based upon human feelings rather than reason.

By discounting religion, he also discounted the virtues of humility as "monkish" and "weakness". He never found enough evidence to accept any religious position, and found religions to be deleterious to human progress. He believed that only human "reasoning" could be relied upon in determining truth. He, like many of his fellow "intellectuals", believed that perfection of "reason" was superior to all human history to date.

His egocentric thought as well as his distaste for humility (as well as its resultant wisdom) can be gleaned from his own quotes:

> "I have no patience for monkish traits – like humility – it is rejected by men of reason because they serve no purpose – don't advance a man's fortune in the world or make one a more valuable member of society. So it is not a virtue, but rather a vice."

> "The superstition that the future resembles the past, is not grounded on arguments of any kind, but is derived entirely from habit."

> "It is not reason which is the guide to life, but custom."

"Any pride of haughtiness is displeasuring to us, merely because it shocks our own pride and leads us by sympathy into comparison which causes the disagreeable passion of humility."

"Weakness, fear, melancholy, together with ignorance are the true sources of superstition. Hope, pride, presumption, a warm indignation, together with ignorance, are the true sources of enthusiasm."

"The bigotry of theology is a malady which seems almost incurable."

"The greater part of mankind may be divided into two classes: that of shallow thinkers who fall short of the truth; and that of obtrusive thinkers who go beyond it."

"The difference between a man who is led by opinion or emotion and one who is led by reason. The former, whether by will or not, performs things of which he is entirely ignorant; the latter is subordinate to no one, and only does those things which he know to be of primary importance in his life, and which on that account he desires the most; and therefore, I call the former a slave, but the latter free."

I would submit that by suppressing humility, he surrendered to arrogance. He never married and claimed no children. When he became fully engaged in deep thought and writing, he experienced what appears to have been a mental breakdown and possibly scurvy. Eventually, he was

THE DECLINE OF HUMILITY AND
THE DEATH OF WISDOM

described as obese, and with a fondness of rich foods and drink. He ultimately achieved the public acclaim he craved and thoroughly enjoyed it. He wrote his own funeral oratory and wished to be buried in a "simple Roman tomb."

Immanuel Kant (1724-1804) was a student of Hume and struggled reconciling his belief in science with his faith. He was born in Prussia into a Lutheran family. He acknowledged that a belief in immortality was essential for humanity to seek high levels of morality, but that human reasoning could not attain real knowledge as to whether God or souls exist or could be understood. He was certainly a true follower of Hume as he moved towards transcendental idealism and placed his human faith solely in reason as well. His quotes best speak for him:

> "All our knowledge begins with senses, proceeds then to understanding and ends with reason. There is nothing higher than reason."

> "Nothing is divine, but what is agreeable to reason."

> In relation to humility – "if a man makes himself a worm, he must not complain when he is trodden on."

> "Immaturity is the incapability to use one's intelligence without guidance of another."

> "Happiness is not an ideal of reason, but of imagination."

> "I had, therefore, to remove knowledge, in order to make room for belief…"

Although Kant lived modestly, and lead a simple and regimented lifestyle, he did not value humility. He placed science and mathematics in high regard but considered the value of human reason to be paramount. It is hard to underestimate the effect Kant's teaching had upon Western philosophical and political thought.

Friedrich Nietzsche (1844-1900) was a German philosopher who essentially took over where Kant left off. Nietzsche was almost vitriolic toward religion, and Christianity in particular. Because Kent refused to absolutely rule out the possibility of an afterlife, or the existence of a creator, Nietzsche referred to him as a religious apologist (not a compliment). Nietzsche expanded his criticisms to traditional European morality and political thought as well. He also attacked secular consciousness, including moral responsibility, guilt for harm to others, altruism, compassion, and any theory of human equality. In fact, he found such moral principles to be potentially harmful.

Most of his writing career was spent attacking contemporary European virtues and pieties, but he didn't produce a set of cogent replacement values until his later work, The Antichrist:

> "What is good? Everything that heightens the feeling of power in man, the will to power, power itself."

> "What is bad? Everything that is born of weakness."

THE DECLINE OF HUMILITY AND
THE DEATH OF WISDOM

> "What is happiness? This feeling that power is growing, that resistance is overcome."

His views toward humility have similarities to those of Kant, but are taken to a cynical extreme:

> "There is a stupid humility that is quite common and when a person is afflicted with it, he is once and for all disqualified from being a disciple of knowledge."

> "God is dead."

> "Humility is a virtue of the slave morality. It is cunning and calculating self-deprecation of the weak, orienting to dominating the strong."

> "He who humbles himself wants to be exalted."

> "The trodden worm curls up. This testifies to its caution. It thus reduces the chances of being trodden upon again. In the language of morality: humility."

Nietzsche did not believe that morality existed in nature, but was the creation of man. He also denied the concept that every human person had intrinsic value, or equality. He believed that certain individuals were "higher" manifesting genuine value, whereas others were of no value at all.

Karl Marx (1818-1883) was born in Prussia into an upper-middle class Jewish family, and his father was a lawyer. Prior to Karl's birth, his father converted, and joined the Evangelical

Church of Prussia because of political developments and increased discrimination against the Jewish people.

As he grew up, Marx became an atheist and engaged in radical left causes which precipitated his move to Paris. He eventually met the German socialist, Freiderich Engles, with whom he became a life-long friend. In collaboration with Engels, he converted his previous ideas of dialectical materialism and historical materialism to what is now known as Marxism. He believed in a worldwide class struggle between the Bourgeoisie and the Proletariat, that Capitalism would eventually create internal tension and struggles which would lead to its self-destruction, and that the perfect socialist state would emerge. His quotes relating to arrogance and the absence of humility make Nietzsche look like a piker:

> "My object in life is to dethrone God and destroy capitalism."

> "The last capitalist we hang shall be the one who sold us the rope."

> "Man makes religion, religion does not make a man."

> "We have no compassion and we ask no compassion from you. When our turn comes, we shall not make excuses for the terror."

> "If you can cut people off from their history, then they can be easily persuaded."

> "Communism begins where atheism begins."

THE DECLINE OF HUMILITY AND THE DEATH OF WISDOM

"The meaning of peace is the absence of opposition to socialism."

"With disdain I will throw my gauntlet full in the face of the world and see the collapse of this pygmy giant. Then will I wander god-like and victorious through the ruins of the world. And giving my words an active force, I will equal the Creator."

Clearly, Marx leaves no room for humility, or the wisdom to be derived from the history of human experience.

Much of his anger and hate may be attributed to the discrimination he and his family experienced when he was growing up, as well as the negative reactions to his writings that caused him to move frequently, and eventually drove him into exile. His health was probably also a factor. He never enjoyed good health, but it seriously deteriorated to what was described as liver and gall disorders, as well as rheumatic pain and chronic skin boils. His bad health understandably led to his famed bad temperament and his cruel and rude behavior toward others.

All four of these writers of philosophy and political thought have had an immeasurable effect on western thought, politics, and history. Clearly, none of them saw any value to humility and all became extremely egocentric, if not narcissistic, they all demonstrated a lack of contentment and happiness. They all suffered from compromised health (from various degrees of self-indulgence), and all were very concerned with their fame and legacy. Their collective unhappiness and negativity may best be described by a few last quotes of Nietzsche:

"Thoughts are the shadows of our feelings - always darker, emptier and simpler."

"The thought of suicide is a great consolation. By means of it one gets through many a dark night."

"Is man merely a mistake of God's? Or God merely a mistake of man?"

This lack of intellectual tolerance, and the lack of appreciation for the value of every individual human life, is the Achilles heel of modern western thought.

The modern applications of Hume's and Kant's reliance upon human reason limits the ability to reach wisdom. By limiting intellectual understanding to sterile applications of inductive and deductive reasoning one must rely upon the "perfection" of the process. Essentially, human reasoning is the creation of human beings, who are by their nature imperfect. Only a delusional human can believe that his reasoning is above human limitations. Humility recognizes critical limitation; modern arrogance overlooks it.

Eastern philosophy has never lost its spiritual dimension – accepting that human beings are an integral part of our environment. We share the majority of our DNA with every other lifeform on this planet. We like to separate ourselves from other members of the animal kingdom by our use of tools, organized language, and cognitive ability. I would contend that man's biggest distinction from other animals is his spiritual nature. He is the only animal that innately

THE DECLINE OF HUMILITY AND
THE DEATH OF WISDOM

understands his own mortality. He acknowledges intuition, inspiration, and love.

Reason is an intellectual exercise; it is not an end in itself. In many ways, modern reason resembles having the best clothes washing machine in the world but neglecting to add water and soap when washing the laundry. No matter how long the washing machine runs, it does not satisfactorily change the state of the dirty clothes. They will remain the same. As Leonard Nimoy once said, " Logic is the beginning of wisdom, not the end."

On the other hand, if you introduce the water of intuition and inspiration, and add the soap of the history of human experience, as well as fabric softener of the wisdom accumulated from others, you can accomplish the goal of actually changing the status of the clothes. Only then can you gain wisdom, as well as the gifts that come from wisdom – especially good judgment.

CHAPTER FIVE

MODERN SOCIETY

"The saddest aspect of life right now is that science gathers knowledge faster than society gathers wisdom."

Isaac Asimov

"The whole problem with the world is that fools and fanatics are always so certain of themselves, and wiser people so full of doubts."

Bertrand Russell (1872-1970)
British Philosopher – logician

"No amount of experimentation can ever prove me right; a single experiment can prove me wrong."

Albert Einstein

"Why do you care so much about laying up the greatest amount of wealth and honor and reputation, and so little about wisdom and truth and the greatest improvements of the soul?"

Socrates

THE DECLINE OF HUMILITY AND THE DEATH OF WISDOM

"The young want massive confidence. The wise avoid it."
Maxine Lagace

"The whole future lies in uncertainty; live immediately."
Seneca

"Too many people believe that everything must be pleasurable in life."
Robert Greene

"Be a master of the mind, not mastered by the mind."
Zen Proverb

"Where there is shouting there is no true knowledge."
Leonardo da Vinci

"Angry people are not always wise."
Jane Austin

"Dogs bark at what they cannot understand."
Heraclitus

The natural progression of the aforementioned modern school of western philosophy is a society dominated by egocentric and arrogant know-it-alls. Many people are convinced that they are the sole possessors of what is right and true. Convinced that they are absolutely right, they never pause to reexamine new information or insight. Civilized discourse has given way to shout-downs.

Popular culture and social media are consumed with celebrity, wealth, power and superficiality. The "Me" generation has evolved into the "Selfie" generation. Image has become more important than reality. Humility is considered to be a weakness relegated to losers. Self-fulfillment is measured by the number of "friends," "likes," or "followers" one has on social media. Photographs are filtered and photoshopped before being posted. Virtual gratification is almost immediate, albeit hopelessly shallow.

Modern society is a culture of materialism and consumption. Obtaining and using material goods is not a problem – in fact, it is probably a necessity of society. However, when accumulating material goods becomes one's sole objective in life, life becomes extremely shallow and meaningless. When obtaining things become more important than how we treat one another, the entire social fabric frays and deteriorates.

When one is deluded into believing that reason alone is sufficient, then one is susceptible to mind games, such as rationalizing. Essentially, virtually anything can be justified in one's mind if rationalization grows unchecked by wisdom. Similarly, people can then justify (in their own minds) uncivilized behavior toward others if it is not tempered by humility.

As people place themselves first, they essentially subjugate everyone else. In other words, if they come first, everyone else must come after them. They then run the risk of losing all social consciousness. Instead of having a healthy society where people rely upon each other's strengths, trust in each other's loyalty, and depend upon each other's compassion, there is an endless competition dominated by "survival of the fittest." Natural philosophy then becomes "the end justifies the means."

A healthy society needs to have shared values and goals, as well as moral principles which guide human conduct. For example, most world civilizations have common principles which have almost universal acceptance – that one should not kill another human being, or steal another's property, or testify falsely against another. Social order normally relies upon people valuing life, respecting property rights, and the need for honest interaction among citizens. In a society dominated by rationalization, these guiding principles can be stretched to the breaking point. Some have come to believe that some lives are more important than others, or that some lives may actually be expendable. Unfortunately, when one life is cheapened, all life is cheapened. History is replete with examples – especially in the 20th century.

Adolf Hitler and his National Socialists developed a theory that the Aryan race was superior to all others, and that certain people were not only inferior, but they were considered a plague on humanity. That rationalization led to some of the worst violations of human rights in world history. The fact that such an evil thought could even be harbored by anyone, let alone spread to an entire modern society, should have been incomprehensible. Unfortunately, it occurred at a terrifying level: approximately 6 million innocent Jews were brutally exterminated in the Holocaust as well as 11 million eastern Europeans, political and religious dissidents, and the "incurably sick." The Second World War which Hitler ignited cost an additional 60 million deaths among soldiers and civilians. Hitler was never accused of being humble nor wise.

The creation of the Soviet Union following the bloody Bolshevik revolution in Russia resulted in the loss of millions of lives as well. Stalin's five-year plans created major disruptions in food production resulting in millions of deaths from famine, as well as the execution of almost a million "enemies of the state" during the Great Purge. The totalitarian regime which ensued continued to engage in a series of executions, mass repressions, and ethnic cleansing which resulted in countless millions of deaths. Stalin and his successors were never accused of being humble or wise.

Not to be outdone, Mao Zedong, an anti-imperialist revolutionary in China, eventually adopted the Marxist and Leninist philosophy. He founded the Chinese Workers' and Peasants Red Army and engaged in a civil war with the Chinese Nationalist Government. Following a short hiatus during World War II when the Chinese factions united to fight against the Imperial Japanese Invasion, Mao Zedong eventually succeeded in defeating the Nationalist Party and drove them into exile in Taiwan. Following the revolution, Mao followed Stalin's example and instituted a bloody consolidation of power and reorganization of China's economy. In addition to the tens of millions of Chinese persecuted during the revolution, and the millions of lives lost in the Korean campaign, his autocratic and totalitarian regime was responsible for the estimated deaths of between 30 – 80 million people through persecution, forced labor, starvation and mass executions. Clearly, those outside of

THE DECLINE OF HUMILITY AND
THE DEATH OF WISDOM

China did not believe Mao or his successors to be humble nor wise.

The three aforementioned regimes are probably the worst examples of genocide, repression and human rights violations in modern history, but they certainly are not the only ones. But they are clear examples of the dangers of arrogance and power when they are not tempered by humility and wisdom. Hitler, Stalin, and Mao were infamous, historically significant, and powerful examples of the egocentric mindset of modern western philosophy. They were clearly "successful" by today's standards of power, wealth, fame, and domination of those who are weaker or deemed inferior.

Many of the same dangers prevalent in modern society are less apparent, but not necessarily less insidious. All one has to do is look around and see how many high-profiled people treat others – especially those who might disagree with them about economics, philosophy, politics or even religion. As I write these words, I know they may sound a little judgmental and I don't wish to make it look as if I am aiming at any particular person, or group of people. That is certainly not my intention.

The traits that I am highlighting are present to some degree in each and every one of us. We all have a propensity to be egocentric or self-centered. We all have some desire for material comfort and happiness. We don't want to be insignificant or consider our lives to be meaningless. At times we are all tempted to take care of ourselves and only those individuals whom we care about.

But every one of us also has the ability to improve ourselves, our outlook and our society. Every one of us has the ability to temper our ego with humility, convert our knowledge to understanding, and our experience to wisdom. More importantly, it is not my desire to judge others, or to have others sit in judgment of one another, but rather for each of us to examine ourself, our own motivations, our personal goals, and our social ethics. That is why it is important to examine our current environment, and how we choose to interface with it.

We live at a time when information is readily available. Science and technology advance at a pace heretofore unknown. That information is available at the touch of a finger or even a voice command on one of our countless devices. However, that knowledge and information can be manipulated by technology as easily as technology is able to bring information to us. Therefore, we need to be vigilant in not allowing information to control us or affect how we choose to treat each other. We must use knowledge and information as a tool to advance our objectives, and not allow the manipulation of information to control our thoughts or actions.

Unfortunately, we are confronted with information and data even when we are not seeking it. We are confronted with news 24/7. We are constantly hit with "pop-ups" when we are on our computers or communication devices. Television shows are interrupted by "breaking news" or unpleasant political commercials. Social media can pull us into a rabbit hole of nasty and vitriolic rhetoric. In fact, we tend to spend more time facing blue screens than we do facing other people in person. We "speak" in texts and memes, rather than spoken

THE DECLINE OF HUMILITY AND
THE DEATH OF WISDOM

words. We tend to talk at people rather than conversing with them as equals.

How often do we engage in active conversations with others? And when we do converse, are those civilized conversations or combative debates? Can we even discuss current events, religion or politics without deteriorating into emotional tirades or name-calling or both? Do our conversations bring ourselves together in commonality, or do they drive us apart by division and derision? Do we approach each other in humility or repel each other with arrogance?

I'm not sure whether politics reflect society or whether society reflects politics, or whether it is a two-way street. But I believe everyone can agree that the current political climate is toxic. The level of discord, vitriol, and unwillingness to compromise has risen to an unprecedented degree. Today's politicians not only attack each other's policies but routinely attack each other personally and sometimes even their family members.

It was not always like this. Alexis de Tocqueville (1805-1859) was a French politician and scientist who travelled to America to study the new Republic. In a series of publications, he praised the division of powers contained in the Federal Constitution, and the level of agreement in principle among its citizenry. In fact, when he studied the two political parties of the time, he commented that the only distinction he could see between them was: one party was in power and the other party was out of power.

What has brought us to this current level of enmity in public discourse, what has effectively changed our national motto from "E pluribus unum" (out of many, one), to "E unum pluribus" (out of one, many)? Instead of a pluralistic society united in guiding principles, our political officials appear to be dividing the public among classifications and pitting one group against another. Instead of respecting each other as individuals, we are encouraged to view each other as members of competing groups. By dehumanizing the groups, it is easier to encourage anger, envy, and even hatred of the label, without concern for the actual human beings behind the label.

At the time de Tocqueville visited the United States, the virtue of humility was universally accepted and honored. In fact, de Tocqueville was particularly impressed by America's incorporation of the virtues brought by the Puritans to New England, and how those virtues, as well as American principles of liberty and equality, were preached throughout all churches in the nation regardless of denomination. However, he also foresaw the potential of these principles unravelling in the future:

> "There are many major principles in both parties in America, but there is no party of principle."

> "There is no country in the world in which everything can be provided for by laws, or which political institutions can prove or substitute for common sense and public morality."

> "Absolute excellence is rarely to be found in any legislation."

THE DECLINE OF HUMILITY AND THE DEATH OF WISDOM

"The American Republic will endure until the day Congress discovers that it can bribe the public with the public's money."

It is almost uncanny that de Toqueville envisioned how we would arrive at our current state.

The modern political stage has no place for humility. The level of hubris in public life would shock even the ancient Greek philosophers. It is hard to remember any recent politicians who sincerely admitted that they were wrong, made a mistake, or were less than honest. Instead, modern politicians accuse their opponents of the same offenses which they themselves are guilty of committing. If they change a position on policy, many deny their earlier statements (even if they have been video recorded) and call their accusers liars (and sometimes much worse). What happened to the quality of tempering ego with acknowledgement of one's human limitations? What happened to owning one's mistakes and learning from them?

Perhaps the biggest problem in Washington, D.C., and probably many state capitals, is the overconfidence and often arrogance, politicians display regarding their position on issues. There is an absolute unwillingness to reexamine positioning even when new evidence and circumstances arise. This often comes from refusing to admit that a previously held position was wrong, or perhaps worse, that a particular person was wrong. The problem becomes even more dire when people avoid challenges by suppressing opposing views. Many believe that the most effective way to win an argument is to make sweeping assertions as to the intentions, motivations, and integrity of those whom they oppose.

Unfortunately, it is an effective way to discount an otherwise valid opposing view – to the detriment of all involved.

Without humility it is virtually impossible to expect wisdom or good judgment in the public arena. In our world of 24/7 news coverage, there is little time for public officials to reflect and ponder, let alone research. Instead, our leaders rely upon "experts." Today, "expertise" appears to be worshipped more than any other form of faith. Most experts, especially those who enjoy being accepted as experts, expect to have their opinions accepted as Gospel without questioning.

Unfortunately, experts are still human beings with all the human limitations and faults that come with being a mere mortal. After 38 years of legal practice as a trial attorney and as a jurist, I have come to realize that you can have experts on both sides of almost every issue. In fact, professional experts can be extremely convincing even when they reach diametrically opposing conclusions. Often experts can carry a degree of academic arrogance that would make Hume and Kant proud. When "experts" testify in a jury trial, jurors are usually given a standard jury instruction to guide them in deciding who to believe, how much to believe, and how much weight should be given to an expert's testimony:

> "An expert is a person who has special knowledge or skill in some science, profession, occupation or subject that the witness acquired by training, education or experience whose knowledge or skill may supply jurors with specialized information, explanations and opinions that will help them decide a case…The fact that such witnesses may be referred to as "experts" does not mean that their testimony

THE DECLINE OF HUMILITY AND
THE DEATH OF WISDOM

and opinions are right. Jurors are required to decide credibility and what weight to give an expert's testimony including the training, education and experience of each expert; the factual information on which he or she based an opinion, the source and reliability of that information, and the reasonableness of any explanation he or she gave to support the opinion." (From Pennsylvania Standard Criminal Jury Instruction 14.0A)

Such an instruction is based upon the collective wisdom of American Jurisprudence spanning centuries of American and British Common Law traditions.

Similarly, we should all treat modern "experts" with the same common-sense analysis. An honest expert would never claim to have 100 percent certainty in an opinion because an imperfect world doesn't provide such certainty. The data and assumptions forming the basis of an opinion can always contain error. Therefore, a better role for an expert is to assist another person in understanding the principles and processes leading to the conclusion in an attempt to give that person confidence in the conclusions. Many modern experts, drawing on academic arrogance demand that their conclusions be accepted (because the expert is obviously smarter and better educated than anyone else.) Unfortunately, politics isn't the only arena where there is a painful lack of humility and wisdom.

CHAPTER SIX

ANXIETY

"Unease, anxiety, tension, stress, worry – all forms of fear – are caused by too much future, and not enough presence."

Eckhart Tolle

"Our anxiety does not come from thinking about the future, but from wanting to control it."

Kahlil Gibson

"Stress and confusion come from being busy. Peace and clarity come from slowing down and stilling your waters."

Maxine Lagace

"If you are distressed by anything external, the pain is not due to the thing itself, but your estimate of it; and this you have the power to revoke at any time."

Marcus Aurelius

THE DECLINE OF HUMILITY AND
THE DEATH OF WISDOM

"To be in harmony with the wholeness of things is not to have anxiety over imperfections."

Dogen Zenji

"Stress is not created by events in your life, but by your reaction to them."

James Pierce

"Problems only exist in the human mind."

Anthony de Mello

"Stop thinking and end your problems."

Lao Tzu

"Compassion and peace of mind bring a sense of confidence that reduce stress and anxiety."

Dalai Lama

"An ignorant state, stress is."

Yoda

Anxiety appears to have reached epidemic proportions in the United States. According to an article in the April 2020 edition of Men's Health, 32 percent of all-Americans report being more anxious now than they were the previous year, and current statistics reflect that 31 percent of U.S. adults will experience an anxiety disorder in their lifetime. Moreover, 48,000,000 prescriptions are written each year for Xanax, an anti-anxiety medication, which doesn't even account for the other types of benzodiazepines - which can all be highly addictive.

Although experts agree that anxiety levels are reported at dramatically increasing rates, there is not a lot of consensus as to the exact cause or causes of that anxiety. Many believe that anxiety is reported more frequently because the stigma of mental health issues has been significantly removed. Others attribute it to the increased hustle of modern society, while others note that the average person is inundated with frightening news as part of the endless 24/7 news cycle. Still others attribute it to unrealistic views people obtain from social media. None of these explanations are mutually exclusive, and a strong case can be made that increased anxiety levels may be the result of a combination of all those factors.

Generally, anxiety is defined as a combination of fear, apprehension, and worry. It is essentially the body's natural response to stress. Normal stress and resulting anxiety is actually healthy. It is the natural survival instinct which can boost awareness and energy in a life-threatening situation. It is often referred to as the natural "fight or flight" response. However, when stress and resultant anxiety continue for an extended period of time, or increase in intensity without a corresponding stimulus, anxiety can cause serious mental and physical harm to one's health.

Fortunately, in modern life there are few truly life-threatening situations, or physical attacks upon us which would require a physical response to actually fight to defend ourselves, or to flee to safety. Instead, most stress in life is created in our own mind. It comes from how we view the world, ourselves, and the relationship between the two. We

THE DECLINE OF HUMILITY AND
THE DEATH OF WISDOM

often become too concerned with how others view us or what they might be thinking or saying about us.

We also tend to place a lot of the world's worries on our own shoulders. We worry about world events, economic concerns, crime, and perhaps, social disruption. We can be obsessed by issues at work, tensions in our family, or friends in crisis. If these worries are purely situational and in direct response to an immediate event, they are completely normal and are manageable because we know that they will resolve themselves sooner rather than later. However, when the worries become constant or chronic, one is at risk of developing an anxiety disorder.

Why has anxiety become such a major societal issue? And why is "anxiety" a chapter in a book on humility and wisdom? There is a clear correlation between the stressors of the modern world and the decline in the value that society places on humility. Humble people often tend to handle stress better than self-centered individuals. Humility helps one to not be overly concerned with what others think or to be worried about self-image. Humility eliminates the belief that one is personally responsible for the world's problems or is charged with finding possible solutions. Unfortunately, the digital world can draw one into its virtual universe where people post photos taken through digital filters. Many exaggerate, if not outright lie, about their lives, extravagant homes, cars, luxurious vacations, professional success, and happiness. Such social media distortion can create angst and worry in people who feel that they cannot measure up to unreachable standards. This problem exacerbates when people spend increasing amounts of time immersing themselves into these platforms.

Social media can also magnify the amount of news (usually negative) one is exposed to. In addition to normal 24/7 news outlets, social media expands that reach. For example, on Facebook everyone has a newsfeed that contains posts and comments from all of one's "friends." Posts may include news or political stories as well as comments on those posts – which often invite additional comments. During political cycles, those commentaries can be extremely vitriolic and stressful. On top of posts, the Facebook platform introduces commercial or political advertisements which an algorithm determined that someone might want to view. Because of crises, real or imagined, with which one is confronted, it is easy for someone to become stressed and worried.

There are many movements and causes that are designed to save the world from natural and man-made calamities. It is hard for someone not to believe that they must act, refrain from acting, support or boycott, protest or contribute, in order to save us all from ourselves. I remember seeing a bumper sticker which read "If you're not outraged you must not be paying attention." It is no wonder that levels of anger, rage, hostility, worry and depression are at unprecedented levels.

Our lives are further complicated by the pace of modern life. According to most European observers, Americans spend too much time working and not enough time enjoying life. Western Europeans have long vacations or holidays while Americans average two weeks of vacation a year, and many are not even taking the vacation available. Many American

THE DECLINE OF HUMILITY AND
THE DEATH OF WISDOM

workers believe that they have a better work ethic than many Europeans, but that may not be the case. American workers log more hours of work, but those longer hours do not necessarily translate into increased productivity commensurate with the extra time invested. In other words, many Americans may work well beyond the point of diminishing returns.

Regardless of the merits of the work ethic/productivity debate, one conclusion is apparent: Americans are less healthy. Americans, especially on the east coast, seem to be caught up in the constant hustle and bustle. They often feel that they are in constant competition with each other in order to get ahead. Many people convince themselves that they can multi-task and, thereby, cram 30 hours of work into each 24-hour day. Even at night and on weekends, Americans are checking emails and returning texts. They are constantly on call for work, and thereby shortchange their families and even themselves.

Americans even tend to drive our children to excel. Parents compete and push their children to reach the landmarks of first words, first steps, first recitation of the alphabet. Believing that pushing them academically and in sports and activities helps them get ahead – to get into more prestigious schools, colleges, professional schools, etc. Even when they succeed in getting children into Ivy League Schools, the students are often on psychotrophic medications to help them cope with all the pressure they feel. Where is it written that a successful life must be a "rat race?"

Eventually, all of these increased levels of angst lead to a revelation that we are not in control of our world or our lives. But control is exactly what popular culture says we should be seeking. After all, we have all of the world's knowledge at our disposal, and we have been told that science and technology can answer all our questions and solve all our problems. And of course, there is nothing that human reason can't solve. We have an abundance of "experts" to guide us to the Promised Land.

The problem intensifies when we realize that when we "solve" one problem, another arises – often a bigger one. For example, we take medication for our anxiety which seems to help resolve the symptoms; however, over time, because the body can create a tolerance to the medication, doses have to be increased to provide the same result. Eventually, that person becomes addicted to benzodiazepine and can't think clearly anymore. Withdrawal from "benzos" is not only difficult but can be dangerous if not done under close medical supervision.

Ironically, while pursuing control, we often lose control. Not only can we not control the world, often we cannot control ourselves. In fact, there are few things we can actually control in life. We cannot control the weather, let alone the planet. We cannot control others – because everyone has free will. We cannot control what life throws at us. About the only thing that we can control is our reaction to what occurs around us. And of course, we can try to control that to which we expose ourselves. We can unplug from the digital world and enjoy the real world for a while. I would suggest that we can draw upon the humble wisdom of others:

> "Just keep in mind: the more we value things outside our control, the less control we have."
>
> Epictetus

THE DECLINE OF HUMILITY AND THE DEATH OF WISDOM

"The need for certainty is the greatest disease the mind faces."
Robert Greene

"People search for certainty. But there is no certainty."
Richard F. Feynman

"Relax, nothing is under control."
Adi Da

"A calm and modest life brings more happiness than the pursuit of success combined with constant restlessness."
Albert Einstein

"Life is a series of natural and spontaneous changes. Don't resist them; that only creates sorrow."
Lao Tzu

"Be more concerned with your character than your reputation, because your character is what you really are, while your reputation is merely what others think you are."
John Wooden

"Humility always begins in our hearts. As a result, it offers significant control over attitude, outlook and actions. It has nothing to prove, but everything to offer."
Joshua Becker

The greatest benefit of wisdom, or good judgment, is perspective. By striving to see the larger picture, to understand what might be happening under the surface, or realize that the present moment is but a small dot on the world's enormously long timeline, we can see that our current problem may not be as significant as we first thought. We are not alone; and therefore, we don't have to solve every dilemma by ourselves. Someone in the past has probably experienced the same issue and may be able to provide insight and guidance.

When we watch the news, we should understand how much the news industry has changed over time. When I was a child, television news was a public service provided by the networks to comply with FCC regulations. The networks rarely made a profit, or even broke even, on the news. Accordingly, news was presented at a bare minimum in order to satisfy the FCC.

As news shows commanded greater viewership, networks could charge greater fees for commercials during the news, and half-hour news shows became hour-long shows, and news shows became more frequent. After the Iran Hostage Crisis started in November of 1979, the special news show "Nightline" began, and eventually became a permanent feature. Similarly, 24-hour news stations soon came into favor. More people began to regularly watch the news than any other type of television programming. News alerts and "breaking news" became routine.

Since bad news seems to sell, almost every tragedy in the country, regardless of distance or magnitude, finds its way into the national news. The result of which is that most people perceive that there is a dramatic increase in crime

THE DECLINE OF HUMILITY AND THE DEATH OF WISDOM

rates, even when crime rates may be on a decline. Despite all of the reported stories, truly wise people realize that these stories need to be viewed in perspective. In a nation with over 320,000,000 inhabitants, there are significant numbers of bad people doing bad things. This is not to diminish the magnitude of tragedies or to minimize the pain endured by those directly affected, but rather to demonstrate that the resultant anxiety and negativity should be placed into better perspective. This is not to make one overly complacent, but instead to make sure the concern raised is proportionate to reality. Concern is normal, but worry is a useless and unhealthy emotion.

Individually, we don't have to solve all the problems of our nation, or the world. If each of us concentrates on our local problems as they directly affect us, our friends, our family, and our communities, the larger problems of our cities, states, nation, and world will most likely diminish as well. We cannot directly affect crime statistics nationally, but we can take reasonable precautions to reduce our local statistics by protecting our family and neighbors by locking the doors to our homes and cars, and by being vigilant in watching our environment at home, in our neighborhoods, at work, and while traveling. Such actions can provide a sense of control over our lives.

By concentrating on things which we can reasonably accomplish, we don't have to stress over things which we cannot accomplish. Instead of obsessing over the one aggressive driver who cut you off, concentrate on the hundreds of drivers around you who operate their vehicle responsibly and courteously. Instead of getting upset by the bad news, imagine all the good news which is occurring and is rarely covered. Perspective puts almost everything in a softer light.

When the virtual world gets too stressful, simply unplug. By doing so, one will realize how much time that has been wasted on social media. One will also realize how rapidly one's disposition and quality of sleep will improve. If, as a result, we find ourselves with more time on our hands, physical exercise and quality face-to-face time with friends and family can easily fill that void. Those activities will provide you with a much better sense of well-being.

By unplugging from technology, one is better able to engage with nature. A walk in the park, forest, or just around the block, can lower anxiety and blood pressure. An escape to the mountains, countryside, or beach can provide an immediate sense of humility and proportionality. Nature has the ability to reboot our souls. As the writer and journalist Edwin Dobbs said in the February 1995 edition of Harper's Magazine:

> "Who has not gazed at the night sky, mouth slightly agape? The experience is so common, its effect so uniform, that a standard vocabulary has evolved to describe it. Invariably we speak of the profound humility we feel before the enormity of the universe. We are as bits of dust in a spectacle whose scope beggars the imagination, whose secrets make a mockery of reason."

THE DECLINE OF HUMILITY AND
THE DEATH OF WISDOM

Once we accept that we are but a temporary inhabitant of an enormous universe, humility is an unavoidable result. Sometimes we just have to take a deep breath and ponder.

If our quest is for certainty in life, we are destined to be forever frustrated. Knowledge is a never-ending process of learning. We must always be willing to reassess the truths we hold when new facts and insights present themselves. When we accept our limitations, and are satisfied by simply doing our best, anxiety gives way to peace of mind:

> "During the flames of controversy, opinions, mass disputes, conflicts and world news, sometimes the most precious, refreshing, peaceful words to hear amidst all the chaos are simply and humbly 'I don't know.'"
>
> Chriss Jami

Caveat: Nothing in this chapter is intended to discourage those diagnosed with an anxiety disorder from seeking and obtaining professional treatment. Severe anxiety is best addressed by appropriately prescribed medications, and/or psycho-therapy – such as cognitive behavioral therapy.

CHAPTER SEVEN

ARROGANCE AND VIOLENCE IN MODERN SOCIETY

"Only an arrogant person thinks they can lie, steal and cheat to get what they want, and never get caught."

Carlos Wallace

"Ego is an illusion of I."

"Arrogance is lifelong ascending madness."

Amit Kalantri

"Arrogance is an illusion of superiority one perpetrates upon their self. Some may ultimately find their way through the illusion, but only after many losses."

Debra Crown

"Arrogance is a self-defense tactic to disguise insecurities."

Caroll Michels

THE DECLINE OF HUMILITY AND THE DEATH OF WISDOM

"Arrogance is blind to the stumbling block."
"Arrogant people beat each other."
Toba Beta

"Arrogance is just another form of selfishness."
Wayne Gerard Trotman

"Arrogance and impulsivity blind the eye of the mind. Humbleness promotes respect and good will. Arrogance invites disrespect and ill will."
Dr. T. P. Chia

"I think that there's something in the American psyche, it's almost this kind of right or privilege, this sense of entitlement, to resolve our conflicts with violence."
Michael Moore

"Arrogance really comes from insecurity, and in the end our feelings that we are bigger than others is really the flip side of our feeling that we are smaller than others."
Desmond Tutu

"It is the certainty that they possess the truth that makes men cruel."
Antole France

"Arrogance makes you stronger from outside, but even weaker from inside."
Ujas Soni

> "The opposite of humility is arrogance – the belief that we are wiser or better than others. Arrogance promotes separation rather than community. It looms like a brick wall between us and those from whom we could learn."
>
> John Thomas Template

As modern western philosophy has succeeded in reducing the role of humility in modern society, popular culture has accepted Hume's premise that humility is not a virtue, but instead a vice. Who has time for perceived weakness when one is chasing fame and celebrity? Who has time for humility when everything is all about me? This egocentric view has an extremely troubling result: as we become increasingly more concerned with ourselves, we became proportionately less concerned about others. If everyone is willing to do what it takes to get ahead, there will be countless victims left in that path of destruction.

As discussed earlier, one of the primary benefits of the wisdom of humility is the respect of others as equals. Removing humility from the public arena changes one's view of others from being equal, dignified human beings, to the role of people who need to be subjugated to our will. The chapter on Hitler, Stalin and Mao demonstrated what happens when humility is removed from rulers; this chapter concentrates on what happens when humility is removed from individuals within a society.

Mankind has always been plagued with charlatans, swindlers, hustlers, and con artists. But the frequency and severity of scams have always been inversely proportional to how effectively pro-social conduct is emphasized by a society.

THE DECLINE OF HUMILITY AND THE DEATH OF WISDOM

Bad conduct is usually discouraged by the fear of being caught, the anticipated punishment for such conduct in life, and atonement in a perceived afterlife.

What happens when people no longer accept a higher authority but come to believe that they are smarter or superior to others (and therefore don't have to answer to anyone for their conduct)? This could be an explanation for the major upsurge in fraud crimes being inflicted upon our citizenry – especially upon the elderly and other vulnerable people. Scammers come by phone, Internet, and in person more frequently than ever before. Victims have had their bank accounts emptied and identities stolen at previously unimagined rates. It defies imagination that human beings can virtually destroy other human beings with no apparent conscience.

If thefts and fraudulent crimes aren't bad enough, the levels of violence related to criminal enterprises are equally alarming. Instead of waiting to steal cars or burglarize homes until no one was around, there is a disturbing increase in the frequency of car-jackings and home invasions. Similarly, there is an unprecedented increase of shootings in many urban areas which may be related to drug disputes. Even when the shootings result in homicides, there is an alarming reluctance for many, including victims and family, to cooperate in the investigations or to testify in court.

There is also a disturbing trend toward increased domestic violence and gang-related shootings. Many people don't place a high value on their own lives, let alone the lives of others. Many prefer to retaliate by resorting to violence themselves rather than assist law enforcement in bringing the perpetrators to justice. Many people believe that they have a right to take justice into their own hands, and brutally seek revenge. To further exacerbate the problem, many using firearms are often not adept at their use, and casualties are frequently innocent bystanders – often referred to as collateral damage.

This arrogant thinking becomes more toxic as people become more withdrawn from interpersonal relationships. Modern people have begun to reduce their circle of friends, often excluding relatives, and view almost everyone else as "outsiders" or the "enemy." This can be rival gangs, those living in different neighborhoods, or those of dissimilar demographics. By grouping people into classifications, people lose their individuality and personal human dignity in the eyes of those doing the "grouping."

As people reduce the number of real-life people with whom they physically interact, they often replace them with virtual people in social media. Those people become more impersonal and undeserving of empathy or sympathy. It's easier to dislike, or even hate, abstract people as opposed to actual people whom they have known or interacted with in person. It becomes easier to consider virtual people inferior, less smart, and less worthy than yourself.

People are naturally wired to communicate in person. Human beings rely a lot on eye contact, body language, and voice inflection to provide necessary clues for better communication, understanding, and bonding. Affection requires actual human connection – human to human interaction. One cannot appreciate human dignity and

THE DECLINE OF HUMILITY AND
THE DEATH OF WISDOM

formulate respect until one can view another as an actual living and breathing being, not merely a social media presence.

As we withdraw from real-time, in-person communication, we miss the opportunity to either validate our thoughts, or listen to where our reasoning might be misguided, or sometimes dangerously wrong. We lose the opportunity to have someone talk us "off the roof." A caring human being has the ability to recognize unhealthy thinking and to either redirect the thinking, or to guide someone to a resource which can provide help. Without that intervention, a troubled egocentric individual will continue to withdraw, isolate, and connect with other disturbed personalities. They may identify enemies and plan retribution. This convergence can be one possible explanation for the phenomenon of the modern mass murderer.

Clearly, one cannot take another human being's life, let alone a number of lives, without having at the core an inflated ego. One must have a sense of superiority and justification to believe that he or she is entitled to end someone else's life. To take a large number of lives, the levels of distain, contempt, and presumptuousness would have to be off the charts. (Of course, one cannot overlook obvious aspects of mental illness and other criminological factors that may have impact in such crimes.)

Some mass murderers defy all explanation, and many have no identifiable motive. However, many seem to be individuals who are viewed as moral outcasts. They may have been severely bullied (or the perpetrators at least believe that they have been severely bulled or ostracized). At some point, their thought process leaves any semblance of humility behind, as well as any sense of societal restraint. The self-indulgent thought moves from the perceived harms done to oneself, toward how that person will hold others accountable. Instead of a laser-focus on a particular target which is apparent in most pre-meditated murder cases, the mass murderer focuses on groups of people with little concern for whether some of the potential targets may be innocent of the perceived indignities. The plan expands beyond the original desire for revenge, to a desire to compensate for one's internal weaknesses by projecting a powerful force upon others (ie: arrogance as a cover for inadequacy). That arrogant thought process may lead to a desire to go out in a "blaze of glory." The actions raise the actor from obscurity to desired fame or infamy. There appears to be a self-absorbed desire to leave a legacy. Unfortunately, too often media coverage provides the notoriety they crave, even if posthumously.

This analysis is purely anecdotal, and not data driven. In fact, although no two mass murderers think exactly alike, the role of arrogance is certainly at play in virtually every case. Even delusional or pathological thought is not void of egocentric obsession. At the very least, there is a complete rejection of humility and wisdom as well as respect for life or social duty.

With humility, we are able to gain control of our ego. When we control our ego, we are less apt to act aggressively or try to manipulate or subjugate others. As a result, we are less likely to behave dishonestly. We can take ownership and responsibility for our mistakes and shortcomings by correcting our mistakes and appropriately modifying our behavior. Perhaps, more importantly, we can actually

THE DECLINE OF HUMILITY AND
THE DEATH OF WISDOM

listen to other people's ideas and gracefully receive constructive feedback. All of this will advance the process of keeping our perception of our talents and abilities in humble perspective.

CHAPTER EIGHT

DRUG ADDICTION

"The mentality and behavior of drug addicts and alcoholics is wholly irrational until you understand that they are completely powerless over their addiction and unless they have structured help they have no hope."

Russell Brand

"In the sixties people took acid to make the world weird. Now the world is weird, and people take Prozac to make it normal."

Damon Albarn

"I guess the worst day I have had was when I had to stand up in rehab in front of my wife and daughter and say, 'Hi, my name is Sam and I am an addict'."

Samuel L. Jackson

"When you can stop, you don't want to, and when you want to, you can't."

Luke Davies

THE DECLINE OF HUMILITY AND THE DEATH OF WISDOM

"Drugs are merely the most obvious form of addiction in our society. Drug addiction is one of the things that undermines traditional values."

Christopher Lasch

"A snapshot feature in USA Today listed the five greatest concerns parents and teachers had about children in the '50s: talking out of turn, chewing gum in class, doing homework, stepping out of line, cleaning their rooms. Then it listed the five top concerns of parents today: drug addiction, teenage pregnancy, suicide and homicide, gang violence, anorexia and bulimia. . . Between my own childhood and the advent of my motherhood--one short generation--the culture had gone completely mad."

Mary Blakely

"One of the things you learn in rehab is that you are responsible for your own actions."

Dale Archer, MD

"Have patience with all things, but chiefly have patience with yourself. Do not lose courage in considering your own imperfections but instantly set about remedying them – every day begin the task anew."

St. Francis de Sales

"I'm not addicted to cocaine. I just like the way it smells."

Richard Pryor

> "Cocaine is God's way of telling you you are making too much money."
>
> Robin Williams

Perhaps the greatest social scourge of our time is drug and alcohol addiction. Today, it would be hard to find anyone who has not been touched by tragedy resulting from drug and/or alcohol abuse. We have experienced unnecessary carnage on our highways from chemically impaired drivers. There are countless impoverished families, where one or both parents suffer from addiction. Perhaps, more disturbing, is the number of fatal opioid overdoses, especially among our youth. What started as a counter-culture movement in the sixties has developed into the worst epidemic of modern times.

The cause or causes of chemical addiction are the subject of much debate. It is most likely a combination of genetic predisposition, cultural acceptance and encouragement, and a set of motivators. The problem is amplified by a cheap and plentiful supply of illicit drugs combined with a large amount of disposable income. Getting a clear picture of causation is complicated by society's obvious need to prioritize the treatment of addiction over academic research into what may be driving addiction. Moreover, the best source of information, the addict, may not even be aware of what caused his or her addiction, or too ashamed to admit the causes because of social stigma. Perhaps even more significant is the percentage of addicts who will not even admit that they are addicts – either to alcohol, drugs, or both.

The magnitude of opioid addiction is particularly clouded by the understandable desire of some families to not disclose

THE DECLINE OF HUMILITY AND
THE DEATH OF WISDOM

the cause of death in obituaries when it is due to an opioid overdose. Often, many do not see addiction as a disease, but rather a personal weakness or a family failure. In court, many heroin addicts try to blame their addiction on prescribed pain medications, only for the court to ultimately learn from family members that they were never prescribed such medications, but rather that they originally obtained them on the street for recreational use. This does not overlook the tragic number of people who indeed become addicted through the lawful use of prescription opioid pain medications, but this information does point out the difficulties researchers have when they try to accurately identify the causes and progressions of addiction.

Referencing the quotation from Dr. Mary Blakely at the beginning of the chapter, there has been an obvious shift in our culture between the 1950's and the present time. What has precipitated this monumental change in our society? Historically, substance abuse has always existed in the world. Even at the time of the American Revolution, there was significant use of opium pipes by many in the upper class, but there was not an epidemic of abuse. There had always been smoking of tobacco and marijuana (practiced by indigenous people who introduced them to the settlers) but never an epidemic. There was a serious concern with alcohol abuse in 1919, which led to the ratification of the 18th Amendment to the U.S. Constitution enacting prohibition. Later, recognizing that it was impractical, if not impossible, to legislate our way out of alcohol abuse, the 21st Amendment was ratified to rescind prohibition and end the "Great Experiment."

If alcohol and drug use and abuse have always been around, it begs the question as to why the problems are now epidemic in magnitude. Why does America, which forbids the drinking of alcohol before the age of 21, suffer from greater levels of alcoholism than Western Europe, which does not impose such restrictions on their youth? Why does our nation, which arguably enjoys one of the best standards of living, has access to the highest levels of education and information, and has unprecedented technology at our disposal, find itself plagued by drug and alcohol abuse at heretofore unimaginable levels? Americans are losing young lives at a faster rate to opioid overdoses than we experienced from battlefield casualties during the Vietnam War. During the Vietnam War, people were marching in the streets demanding an end to it, but society seems to accept the body count from heroin with hardly a whimper.

Part of this problem can be attributed to the decreasing levels of humility and wisdom in our society. As people become more egocentric, they begin to believe that they have a right to feel good, and to avoid pain and discomfort. They convince themselves that they know more than their parents or grandparents, and that they certainly know more about themselves than anyone else. Similarly, as a society, people have become very good at rationalizing and shifting blame. People believe that they are in control of themselves, their addictions, and their lives. Arrogance will not allow them to accept criticism or advice from others. They fail to see how their behaviors, including their addictions, effect those around them – especially those about whom they care most.

THE DECLINE OF HUMILITY AND
THE DEATH OF WISDOM

People rarely consider the cost that their addictions inflict upon society in general.

Humility would allow people to better evaluate themselves and restart the process of improvement. Humility would allow people to learn from others both by their words and their examples. Listening to the stories of others provides perspective that comes with wisdom. Humility would also create an honest empathy for others and provide insight as to how selfish conduct deeply hurts the ones we love.

I have to confess that I am particularly disturbed by what is occurring with heroin addiction. I not only know personal friends who have died from overdoses, but I also have too many friends who have lost children to overdoses. Opioid addiction has no demographic or cultural boundaries. Even in court, most drug cases involve heroin, fentanyl, or other opiates. Today, the vast majority of addicts appear to be addicted to opioids.

One case had a particularly strong effect upon me. A 19-year-old defendant came to court for a revocation hearing claiming that he was clean and taking Vivitrol (Naltrexone) to avoid relapse. Unfortunately, it became apparent that he was under the influence of heroin in court, and when pressed, he admitted that he had not been taking Vivitrol, and that he scored a heroin purchase the previous night while his parents thought he was attending a Narcotics Anonymous meeting. When I was required to detain him until we could find an inpatient treatment bed for him, he literally begged me not to detain him until the next day so he could attend his friend's funeral who had overdosed earlier in the week. When I asked him how many friends he has lost to overdoses, his reply shocked me. He said, "Close friends – six." The magnitude of the problem immediately hit me like a ton of bricks.

Opioid addiction not only enveloped much of his circle of friends, but he allowed himself to relapse and shoot up within days of the overdose death of his sixth close friend. With this addiction there is no thought process involved; it completely overrides reason and will. It is a demon that cannot be fully comprehended. Obviously, he and his young six friends did not all become addicted as a result of being prescribed opioids for pain.

Ironically, as I was writing this chapter, I learned of another defendant in one of my active cases who had just overdosed. He had successfully completed a 14-month inpatient/outpatient program and appeared to be doing well, but unexpectedly relapsed and died. It was even more disturbing to learn that the young man was a classmate and friend of one of my daughters. How can a seemingly normal young person descend into chemical dependency to the point of shooting street heroin into his veins? When someone scores heroin on the street, there is no way of knowing the concentration of the contents, or whether it contains fentanyl which is a synthetic opioid approximately 50-100 times stronger than heroin.

I share the perspective of Dr. Mary Blakely by being a child of the 1950's and remember attending drug education classes in the 1960' and 1970's. In those classes, heroin was described as the "end of the road" for life-long addicts. They were portrayed as elderly (looking back they must have been in their mid-50's) street people who overdosed and died in street gutters. Unfortunately today, heroin abuse and death tends to disproportionately affect young people – regardless of economic means. Why are young, talented individuals with potentially bright futures, finding themselves addicted to such lethal substances? That is probably the million-dollar question.

It is conceivable that the modern hectic lifestyle has increased the prevalence of anxiety and depression to the point where many people self-medicate. It is conceivable that the breakdown in family structure has left many youth without hands-on parental supervision, or that some preoccupied parents prefer to give their children money in lieu of their time. It could be that drug use is highlighted, if not glorified, in social media and in popular music. It could be increased peer pressure to fit in and to be perceived as being cool. It could be that some youth have undiagnosed psychological disorders which lead them to believe that life is too painful to face sober. It could be that kids start drinking alcohol or smoking pot at a young age and develop a disrespect for the laws that prohibit it. Perhaps the early use of drugs/alcohol triggers genetic predispositions for chemical addiction. It is probably a combination of these factors, as well as many that are not listed.

Undoubtedly there is a degree of arrogance involved. Most alcohol and drug abusers believe that they can handle it. Even when alcohol and drug use starts to disrupt life and jeopardize health, the chemically dependent person is usually overly confident that they can control it, and that they know better than friends and family members who confront them. Regardless of how someone becomes addicted to drugs or alcohol, humility is clearly an essential element for successful recovery.

Despite the existence of numerous courses of treatment available for chemical dependency, none of them can work if the addicts are unwilling to acknowledge their problem and actively invest in a course of treatment. For example, it is not uncommon for a criminal defendant to agree to inpatient treatment in order to avoid a more severe sentence. However, just because someone is in an inpatient treatment program doesn't mean that they will actively engage. Even the best inpatient treatment programs require the individual to desire to get better and to be willing to change his or her behavior.

Often addicts go through the motions biding their time and "playing along" with the treatment until they can get out and use again. Others may be convinced that they need to stop using, but feel that they can do it without formal intervention. Many are arrogant enough to believe that they can complete formal treatment, and then use what they've learned in order to control their use once they are on their own. There are countless accounts of addicts who repeatedly complete treatment programs, only to relapse again. These accounts have led to the often-repeated cliché: "Relapse is part of recovery."

As our nation's courts have tried to grapple with this problem, there has been a move toward evidence-based "problem-solving courts" or "treatment courts." I have had the honor of overseeing our county's Veteran's Court, a problem-solving court created on the model of drug court, but specially adapted for Veterans. Our court is directed by a treatment team, including experienced people with

THE DECLINE OF HUMILITY AND
THE DEATH OF WISDOM

different treatment specialties, specialized probation officers, a Veterans' Treatment Coordinator, and dedicated attorneys from the District Attorney's Office and the Public Defender's Office. A very important addition used only in the Veterans' Court are veteran mentors individually assigned to each participating veteran. The mentor coordinator actually sits as a member of the treatment team.

Despite all of the treatment expertise and rehabilitation resources available to us there is one element that has proven to be indispensable for those participating veterans with chemical dependency issues – Alcoholics Anonymous, Narcotics Anonymous, or a comparable 12-step program. These programs do not replace treatment, but rather complement it. Treatment provides the tools necessary for one to learn to abstain from drugs and alcohol; however, it is the 12-step program which provides the community and programming support to help them maintain their sobriety. What I find most profound in the AA/NA program is that, at its core, it is built on the foundation of humility.

As a practicing attorney, I had always been aware of these programs, and appreciated how important they were for people in recovery, but I never bothered to learn how important these programs actually were. I only knew that 12-step programs were to be ordered as part of any successful treatment regimen. I was surprised when our mentor-coordinator approached me with a copy of the AA "Big Book" and suggested that if I was going to be ordering AA/NA for people on supervision, I might want to learn about the program. I was pleasantly surprised at how insightful and helpful that was.

But my real "ah-ha" moment was when I accepted the honor of attending the Eastern Pennsylvania General Service Assembly Convention for Alcoholics Anonymous as their "official observer." It was probably one of the most profound educational experiences of my life. I went there with a certain degree of trepidation – the idea of spending an extended weekend at a convention in Gettysburg with a large group of alcoholics in recovery was hard to imagine. In fact, I fully expected to be surrounded by grumpy old people, and I was practically plagued by the thought of a long convention without a hospitality room or even a glass of wine or a beer at dinner.

To my pleasant surprise, I encountered the most inspirational and diverse group of individuals who were genuinely happy and enthusiastic. There was a surprisingly large number of young people in their teens and twenties, as well as from every other age group. There were people of diverse backgrounds, including gender identity, lifestyles, and faiths (including avowed agnostics). To my amazement, there was complete acceptance of each other without any hint of judgment, although they probably wondered why a judge was in attendance. Everyone was genuinely excited to be in each other's company and to share their passion for a life of recovery.

What became immediately apparent was that everyone there was completely humble. They were honest about their diseases and candid about their experiences on their respective roads to recovery. In fact, every time a speaker began, he or she would state: "Hi, my name is____, and I'm an alcoholic." Everyone was anxious to listen, in a fully open and engaged

THE DECLINE OF HUMILITY AND
THE DEATH OF WISDOM

manner. All of the people present were representing their respective meeting groups, and had completed all twelve steps of the program and were continuing to work the steps and give back to others.

When I learned about the 12 steps, I was amazed at the level of humility and wisdom contained therein. The first step is: "1, We admitted we were powerless over alcohol - that our lives became unmanageable." Such an admission of humility is so contrary to our current culture. However, as most people familiar with the recovery process would concede, humility forms the basis for the need to learn and change. At all times, humility and honesty with oneself and others is essential to successful sobriety. As soon as someone becomes too self-confident and falls victim to the arrogance of "I can control my addiction", that person is destined to fail.

The next two steps build on step one: "2. Came to believe that a Power greater than ourselves could restore us to sanity. 3. Made a decision to turn our will and our lives over to the care of God as we understood Him." At first I was concerned that many people would be initially turned off by what appeared to be a strong religious dimension – which concerned me as a trial judge who is required to maintain secular objectivity in any course of treatment ordered by a court.

In one of the workshops I attended, the AA members emphasized the phrase "…God as we understood Him", and explained that it did not mean any particular religion or in fact any religion at all. "God" could be the force of nature, collective humanism, the "force" from Star Wars, or anything else that the alcoholic could recognize as superior to himself or herself. In other words, there was no need to identify a deity, but rather a need to acknowledge a higher power – whatever or whomever that might be. One attendee told me that she entered AA as an avowed atheist, and that after witnessing the power present in her meetings and more importantly, in her recovery, she now considers herself somewhere between agnostic and a believer in a cosmic material force (ie. nature). It eventually became apparent to me that describing the exact nature of God as He is understood, is less important than acknowledging that a higher power exists. It is the existence of a higher power that allows one to fully embrace humility. Then, it is that humility which allows one to learn and to change.

Once the spirit of humility is established, the next four steps involve the hard work necessary to honestly examine oneself, one's shortfalls, one's past mistakes, and the harm one has done to others: "4. Made a searching and fearless moral inventory of ourselves. 5. Admitted to God (as we understand Him), to ourselves and to another human being the exact nature of our wrongs. 6. We're ready to have God (as we understand Him) remove all the deficits of character. 7. Humbly asked Him to remove our shortcomings." Obviously, anyone who is arrogant would find these steps not only intolerable, but probably impossible. In fact, conceit always gets in the way of someone honestly evaluating the true extent of their shortcomings.

If the previous four steps were not difficult enough, the next two are even more challenging: "8. Made a list of all persons we had harmed and became willing to make amends to them all. 9. Made direct amends to such people whenever possible, except when to do so would injure them or others."

THE DECLINE OF HUMILITY AND THE DEATH OF WISDOM

For someone with a lifetime of addictions, compiling a comprehensive list of everyone that may have been harmed by his selfish lifestyle would be a Herculean task. Then, making amends would probably tax the humblest person to his limits. These difficult tasks certainly add clarity to the phrase "working the steps of Alcoholic Anonymous."

The last three steps appear to help the individual develop the necessary skills and practices for a lifetime of sobriety: "10. Continued to take personal inventory and when we were wrong, promptly admitted it. 11. Sought through prayer and meditation to improve our conscious contact with God as we understood Him, praying only for knowledge of His will for us and the power to carry that out. 12. Having had a spiritual awakening as the result of these steps, we tried to carry this message to alcoholics and to practice these principles in all our affairs."

The final three steps transform humility into wisdom. The reason I say that is because the weekend I spent with those hundreds of alcoholics was truly life changing. When the weekend was over, I was saddened by the thought that I would probably never see most of these amazing people again. I almost wished that I was an alcoholic so that I could join their organization and continue to be in their company. But, alas, I must not have inherited the genetic predisposition to be an alcoholic, because I certainly had ample opportunity to become one. In case anyone is wondering, the hospitality room was awesome. It may not have had alcohol, but it had enough ice cream, candy, and cookies that I never even missed the beer or a glass of wine with dinner.

There are other 12-step programs available as well. There is Narcotics Anonymous, (virtually identical to Alcoholics Anonymous but especially suited for the unique challenges of drug addictions) as well as "smart recovery" and other non-faith-based programs. However, they are rooted in humility and are designed to lead to the wisdom which can allow someone to successfully refrain from alcohol and other drugs. Almost every treatment specialist agrees that formal treatment and counseling for chemical dependency (and sometimes incorporating treatment for related psychological issues) combined with invested participation in a 12-step-recovery community, provides the best chance of success against addiction. However, until someone is humble enough to seek and accept help, it can't happen.

> "You really can't just take someone who's got a drug addiction and just put 'em in rehab. It doesn't work that way. You can't choose it for them. They have to choose it for themselves – because that's scary. It's really hard.
>
> Rosario Dawson

> "I have absolutely no pleasure in the stimulants in which I sometimes so madly indulge. It has not been in the pursuit of pleasure that I have periled life and reputation and reason. It has been the desperate attempt to escape from torturing memories, from a sense of insupportable loneliness and a dread of some strange impending doom."
>
> Edgar Allen Poe

THE DECLINE OF HUMILITY AND THE DEATH OF WISDOM

"Life is very interesting…in the end, some of your greatest pains become your greatest strengths."

Drew Barrymore

CHAPTER NINE

THE PANDEMIC OF 2020

"The ultimate measure of a man is not where he stands in moments of comfort and convenience, but where he stands at times of challenge and controversy."

Dr. Martin Luther King, Jr.

"Expect trouble as an inevitable part of life and when it comes, hold your head high, look it squarely in the eye and say, 'I will be bigger than you. You cannot defeat me. Then repeat to yourself the most comforting of all words: This too shall pass.'"

Ann Landers

"Life is thickly sewn with thorns. I know no other remedy than to pass rapidly over them. The longer we dwell on our misfortunes, the greater their power to harm us."

Voltaire

THE DECLINE OF HUMILITY AND THE DEATH OF WISDOM

"To every obstacle oppose patience, perseverance and soothing language."
Thomas Jefferson

"Adversity, if for no other reason is of benefit, since it is sure to bring a season of sober reflection. People see clearer at such times. Storms purify the atmosphere."
Henry Ward Beecher

"These are times that try men's souls."
Thomas Paine

"Only in winter can you tell which trees are truly green. Only when the winds of adversity blow can you tell whether an individual or a country has steadfastness."
John F. Kennedy

"In times like these, it helps to recall that there have always been times like these."
Paul Harvey

"Think of adversity not so much as a threat to our peace of mind but rather as the very means by which patience is attained."
Dalai Lama

"What worries you, masters you."
John Locke

"The darkest hour has only sixty minutes."
Morris Mandel

> "Turn your face to the sun and the shadows fall behind you."
>
> Charlotte Whitton

> "Courage is being scared to death, but saddling up anyway."
>
> John Wayne

> "If you're going through hell, keep going."
>
> Winston Churchhill

> "The reward of suffering is experience."
>
> Aeschylus

> "Hope is important because it can make the present moment less difficult to bear. If we believe that tomorrow will be better, we can bear a hardship today."
>
> Nhat Hanh

As I am finishing the writing of this book, I am under a stay-at-home order from our Governor related to the Coronavirus (COVID-19) crisis. As this event has unfolded, my observations led me to change the subject of this chapter to the Pandemic of 2020.

The world appears to be changing dramatically all around us, and it is fascinating to see how our country and my state in particular, are responding. I see so many examples of humility and wisdom among so many people, then with others – not so much.

THE DECLINE OF HUMILITY AND THE DEATH OF WISDOM

The events unfolded rapidly with little time for anyone to completely grasp the scope and magnitude of the situation. To make matters worse, the country is heading into a Presidential election year with seemingly unprecedented degrees of contentiousness and outright vitriol. At a time of crisis, most Americans would expect their elected officials would put political disagreements behind them and place the well-being of the nation on the top of all priority lists.

Much information flowed in from China, the World Health Organization, various European countries which were especially hard hit, our own Center for Disease Control and Prevention, and just about every politician and news organization. To say that information was fluid would be an understatement.

Amazingly, most Americans were willing and able to social distance and self-isolate in order to protect fellow citizens who were particularly vulnerable to the ravages of the disease. Americans appeared to be extremely sympathetic to the concerns of the medical profession as to the perceived risk of overwhelming our nation's hospitals and healthcare providers. With great humility, most Americans chose to err on the side of caution and accept the most frightening projections from international and national experts and their respective "models." Instead of challenging the validity of the data or the assumptions of the models, citizens accepted the necessary individual restrictions for the benefit of society as a whole.

On the other hand, many Americans showed a darker side. For some reason, a fraction of the people saw the need to go to the stores and hoard food, cleaning supplies and of all things, toilet paper with little concern for anyone else. There really was no shortage of anything until the fearful made a run on the stores in a manner reminiscent of the Great Depression when there was a run on the banks. In both cases fear, without wisdom, created panic. Hoarding demonstrated personal selfishness rather than concern for the well-being of others.

In similar displays of self-centeredness, others completely discounted the risks (without necessarily doing any personal research) and took advantage of inexpensive airfares by traveling to future hotspots such as New Orleans, Florida, and New York City. Those gatherings placed large numbers of people from disparate geographic areas in close proximity to each other, and the ultimate return to their hometowns with an unexpected souvenir – "the virus."

To further compound the problem, universities and colleges closed, some before, some during, and some after their respective "Spring Breaks." Not surprisingly, many college students acted as typical college students by going to bars and celebrating in close proximity to each other and with foreign students returning from Asia and Europe and then dispersing across the country. Although many students attending spring break in Florida were vilified by the media for their behavior and laissez-faire attitude toward the evolving Pandemic, they were representative of a much larger segment of society who did not take the matter seriously (possibly because of a number of previous false alarms regarding earlier viruses such as the swine flu, SARS, etc.) and engaged in what would be reviewed in hindsight as irresponsible. Again, more self-centered (rather than humble) behavior was on display for all to see.

Eventually, the medical and scientific experts came to the forefront and predicted an apocalyptic projection of mass illness and deaths which would overwhelm all America's hospitals and jeopardize all civilized order. The example of Italy certainly gave credence to such a possibility – especially before learning why Italy was so disproportionately infected by the disease. Then there was a mad dash for governors and mayors to impose their own draconian restrictions to avoid the spread of this disease within their respective jurisdictions.

In a previous chapter, we discussed "experts," and their respective benefits and limitations. Unfortunately, the scientific models developed by some of our most prestigious research universities, backed by our nationally renowned medical experts, all told us to expect a calamity beyond comprehension. Of course, I am not an expert, and I am not criticizing anyone's initial research or projections. What I am questioning is why the experts didn't have their own reservations as to the certainty of their conclusions, and why they didn't revisit their data and assumptions when the models were not playing out as originally expected. It reminds me of a quote by the British professor, medical doctor, and scientist, Baron Robert Winston, M.D.:

> "I think scientific arrogance really does give a great degree of distrust. I think people begin to think that scientists like to believe that they can run the universe."

I don't question our mayors or governors for wanting to take appropriate steps to stop the spread and "flatten the curve," of the disease. However, I do question why they did not proceed in a measured fashion, collaborating with the peoples' legislative representatives, and acting with some deference to the inalienable rights of the citizenry. Unilaterally closing down all "non-essential" businesses and placing the entire population under extended house arrest has never occurred in this country before, and hopefully will never happen again.

The closest example in history, but to a smaller magnitude, was the involuntary detention of all Japanese Americans during World War II. It was done to "save American lives" and protect our nation during that time of war. Perhaps most embarrassing to the legal profession, the United States Supreme Court held at the time that such a detention was "Constitutional" despite the absence of due process and the lack of any misconduct on the part of the detainees. Since that time, almost all legal scholars agree that it was clearly an unconstitutional act which should not have been allowed to occur then nor to be allowed to occur again. The lesson to be learned is that a short-term crisis should never be used to do long term damage to our Constitutional principles.

Again, it is not the goal of this book to question the actions of anyone, but to encourage everyone to act with humility and compassion for each other. Are we acting with empathy and compassion for everyone? Are we treating each other as equals? Are we representing the will of the people, or are we imposing our will upon them? Are we acting wisely and with prudent, good judgment? Are we acting for the greater good of all, or are we advancing our own economic or political

THE DECLINE OF HUMILITY AND
THE DEATH OF WISDOM

agendas? Everyone must search their own hearts and souls for answers to these questions.

One might also question whether it was wise to use a one-size-fits-all approach to this crisis. Should rural communities have been treated the same as urban communities, or should communities with few cases and no deaths have been treated the same as communities overwhelmed by illnesses and deaths? Should the accepted community of experts be expanded to allow greater collective wisdom? Should legislators play a greater role or should chief executives have unfettered authority? Are the national and state constitutions effectively suspended, and if so, for how long, and who should decide how long?

Nationally, how much thought and wisdom went into the emergency legislation? Was there collective wisdom, or did leadership broker a deal at the top? How confident were the economic experts in their assumptions relative to borrowing and printing trillions of dollars without any corresponding productivity? Are there concerns for inflation, and if significant inflation occurs, will interest rates have to go up and thereby choke any economic recovery? Will there be an enormous national debt which cannot be paid by even our great-grandchildren? I don't know the answers to these questions, but I also haven't heard anyone asking them or receiving answers from all the "experts."

Perhaps I would be a little more confident if I knew that our lawmakers were involved in the process, doing their own individual due diligence and fully understanding the magnitude of their endeavors. However, it happened so fast, with no public debate, at a time when the majority of our lawmakers were not even in Washington. More unsettling, there is no record of who voted for or against the largest spending bill in the history of our country. I'm not suggesting that everyone had to be in the Capitol Building, but everyone could have called in, "Zoomed" in, or logged in and registered their formal vote. Their absolute reluctance to do so leaves me much less confident in the result. Why would lawmakers not want to publicly document their vote on such a significant piece of legislation? All of this brings to mind the words of Ross Perot:

> "The budget should be balanced, the treasury should be refilled, the public debt should be reduced and the arrogance of public officials should be controlled."

When our nation was founded, our founders were rooted in humility and wisdom. They didn't always agree, and their arguments were often heated. But they always put the nation's interests above their own. In fact, they risked everything including their lives, families, and fortunes during the Revolutionary War. Accordingly, they designed a Constitution which would protect the people from tyranny by carefully dividing and balancing power. They established a government structure which depended upon people of virtue and good character to govern. In the words of Abraham Lincoln:

> "Nearly all men can stand adversity, but if you want to test a man's character, give him power."

People of good character will carefully use their power and not abuse it.

THE DECLINE OF HUMILITY AND
THE DEATH OF WISDOM

It must be noted here that this chapter is not aimed at anyone. In fact, humility and the search for wisdom is an individual endeavor. Each of us must examine our own humility, and honestly evaluate our own motivations, as well as our own sincerity, in the pursuit of wisdom. In judging someone else's humility, we essentially forfeit our own humility. However, when it comes to questions of wisdom or the exercise of good judgment, that is an appropriate subject for examination and debate. But that examination must be done honestly and impersonally. We must be objective when we examine the actions and results of another's judgment, but not be judgmental of each other.

My firmest hope is that when this book goes to press, the Pandemic of 2020 will be a fading memory and that normality will be returning. I hope our nation as a whole will have exercised the virtues of humility and perseverance with this medical challenge, and that we will have treated each other with equality, empathy, compassion, and respect. I trust that our leaders will have put their country, state, and community above their own personal interests and that they will have willingly and openly recognized any mistakes that may have been made, and taken steps to correct them. Most importantly, I hope everyone was able to gain wisdom by learning not only from what worked, but also from what didn't work, so that we might better address whatever the future holds for us.

> "The truth is that our finest moments are more likely to occur when we are feeling deeply uncomfortable, unhappy, or unfulfilled. For it is only in such moments, propelled by our discomfort, that we are

likely to step out of our ruts and start searching for different ways or truer answers."

M. Scott Peck

"Be generous in prosperity, and thankful in adversity. Be worthy of the trust of thy neighbor, and look upon him with a bright and friendly face. Be a treasure to the poor, an admonisher to the rich, an answerer of the cry of the needy, a preserver of the sanctity of thy pledge. Be fair in thy judgment, and guarded in thy speech. Be unjust to no man, and show all meekness to all men. Be as a lamp unto them that walk in darkness, a joy to the sorrowful, a sea for the thirsty, a haven for the distressed, an upholder and defender of the victim of oppression. Let integrity and uprightness distinguish all thine acts. Be a home for the stranger, a balm to the suffering, a tower of strength for the fugitive. Be eyes to the blind, and a guiding light unto the feet of the erring. Be an ornament to the countenance of truth, a crown to the brow of fidelity, a pillar of the temple of righteousness, a breath of life to the body of mankind, an ensign of the hosts of justice, a luminary above the horizon of virtue, a dew to the soil of the human heart, an ark on the ocean of knowledge, a sun in the heaven of bounty, a gem on the diadem of wisdom, a shining light in the firmament of thy generation, a fruit upon the tree of humility."

Bahá'u'lláh

CHAPTER TEN

RESTORING HUMILITY TO MODERN SOCIETY

"When you are offended at any man's fault, turn to yourself and study your own failings. Then you will forget your anger."

Epictetus

"Those who profit (learn) from adversity possess a spirit of humility and are, therefore, inclined to make the necessary changes needed to learn from their mistakes, failures and losses....When we are focused too much on ourselves, we lose perspective. Humility allows us to regain perspective and see the big picture...Humility allows us to let go of perfection and keep trying."

John. C. Maxwell

"It's amazing what you can accomplish if you don't care who gets the credit."

Harry S. Truman

"To seek the truth requires one to ask the right questions. Those void of truth never ask about anything because their ego and arrogance prevent them from doing so. Therefore, they will always remain ignorant. Those on the right path to Truth are extremely heart-driven and childlike in their quest, always asking questions, always wanting to understand and know everything — and are not afraid to admit they don't know something. However, every truth seeker does need to breakdown their ego first to see Truth. If the mind is in the way, the heart won't see anything."

Suzy Kassem

"Humility is the true key to success. Successful people lose their way at times. They often embrace and overindulge from the fruits of success. Humility halts this arrogance and self-indulging trap. Humble people share the credit and wealth, remaining focused and hungry to continue the journey of success."

Rick Pitino

"Be the peace you want to see in the world."

Dr. Martin Luther King Jr

"To possess self-confidence and humility at the same time is called maturity."

Jack Welch

THE DECLINE OF HUMILITY AND THE DEATH OF WISDOM

> "Winners compare their achievements with their goals, while losers compare their achievements with those of other people."
>
> Nido Quebein

> "The proud man can learn humility, but he will be proud of it."
>
> Mignon McLaughlin

> "You cannot be truly humble unless you truly believe that life can and will go on without you."
>
> Mokokoma Mokhonoana

> "The trouble with most of us is that we would rather be ruined by praise than saved by criticism."
>
> Norman Vincent Peale

Although humility has fallen into apparent disrepute in today's popular culture, it has not disappeared from human experience. Humble people have always been present, but it is hard to hear their whispers over the yelling of modern social media, movies, and television. They obviously don't normally hang out with the rich and famous, or with the powerful. However, if you were to encounter a humble person, and take the time to converse with him or her, you would most likely be drawn to their character, even though you may not identify their qualities as humility.

> "The meek are positive and often colorful characters. They are not self-assertive nor self-seeking, to be sure, but rather they are unselfish and uncomplaining,

> genuinely interested in the welfare of others, creating opportunities to be of service to them, submissive in the face of injuries and insults, silent in the accidents and adversities of life, and bearing with equanimity the infamies and injustices heaped upon them."
>
> V. Raymond Edman

Because humble people are not self-assertive, nor seeking the spotlight, they usually go unnoticed even when their good works are observed.

Humility is the essential building block of constructive social interaction. I would submit that it is the natural state of being human. As children we all start out with minds open to knowledge and hearts open to truth and love. Children respond naturally to kindness and crave attention. They have an inherent awareness of that which they do not know and an almost unquenchable desire to learn and understand. Asking questions (sometimes unceasingly) comes naturally to them, and they feel no embarrassment by what they do not already know.

When humility develops a thirst for knowledge, the humble student becomes much more "teachable." Curiosity provides additional motivation to read and study. That thirst expands beyond knowledge of facts and moves into understanding and the appreciation that understanding is not an end result. Instead, understanding is a process requiring constant reflection and reexamination – especially when circumstances change and/or additional information becomes available. The greatest gift of understanding is the resultant appreciation of all that one has yet to know or understand.

THE DECLINE OF HUMILITY AND THE DEATH OF WISDOM

The humble mindset improves one's ability to relate to others. It allows one to see the intrinsic value of others – their dignity as fellow human beings on the journey of life together. If you can connect with and relate to others, you are in a better position to share information, insight, and understanding, leading to mutual respect and appreciation. Perhaps the deepest desire of each of us is to be appreciated. Appreciation naturally leads to gratitude, and gratitude is a major factor in improving one's attitude and world view.

A basic tenant of the Jewish faith is gratitude. As a people, Jews have an inherent appreciation for their role as "God's chosen people." They respond with constant prayers of thanks to God and share that gratitude with each other. That humility, or fear of the Lord, and the resultant gratitude, was described in the six characteristics of the Spirit of the Lord in Isaiah 11:1-2: "wisdom, understanding, counsel, might, knowledge, and fear of the Lord." Their gratitude grew with God's intervention in freeing his chosen people from captivity in Egypt and delivering them to the Promised Land. No wonder practicing Jews express prayers of gratitude upon awaking, and in prayer throughout the day.

The Jewish principles of humility and gratitude are central to practicing Christians as well. The Roman Catholic Church recognizes the "Seven gifts of the Holy Spirit" as: "wisdom, understanding, counsel, fortitude, knowledge, piety and fear of the Lord." For Catholics, morning, daily and evening prayers are centered on humble piety and gratitude. In fact, the Church's central sacrament of community, the celebration of Christ's last Passover dinner, is referred to as the "Eucharist" (the Greek term for Thanksgiving).

Even in the secular world, a "thank you" goes a long way in conveying appreciation and uplifting moods, especially when accompanied by a smile. Thanks conveys gratitude for a gift or courtesy freely given from human to human. It is not only polite; it is healthy. Gratitude reduces stress and strengthens bonds between people. It is equally as beneficial for the person expressing the gratitude as it is for the person receiving the expression of gratitude.

Starting in 1986, a longitudinal study was commenced at the University of Minnesota and concluded at the University of Kentucky exploring the health effects of gratitude, contentment, love, and hope. It traced approximately 700 nuns from the 1930's until the end of the century. Because they had completed entry questionnaires and continuously journaled their outlooks and attitudes, and they all lived in the same controlled environments (the Schools of the Sisters of Notre Dame), scientists had a perfect sampling to analyze. The study concluded that positive emotions increased their life expectancy by seven years as well as reduced the likelihood of health challenges such as Alzheimer's Disease.

> "In every class of society, gratitude is the rarest of human virtues."
>
> Wilke Collins (1824-1889)
> English Novelist & Playwright

> "Better to lose count while naming your blessings than to lose your blessings to counting your troubles."
>
> Maltbie Davenport Babcock

THE DECLINE OF HUMILITY AND THE DEATH OF WISDOM

I would submit that an equally important byproduct of humility is empathy. Humility allows you to see beyond yourself, and to respect and understand other human beings. By realizing how similar we are, and how similar our experiences and emotions often are, we have the capacity to connect and actually feel what others may be feeling. By experiencing shared pain, we can better understand why someone may have spoken or acted in the manner in which they did. It helps us to avoid misinterpreting others' intentions or motivations. It encourages sharing and enables us to better understand others, as well as better understand ourselves.

Empathy then opens the door to magnanimity, where we find it easier to be forgiving and generous with others. It allows us to be greater in mind and heart, and to dwell in calmness rather than aggression. By better understanding the complexity and humanity of others, we better understand our own complexity and humanity. In time, these qualities lead to equanimity and an ability to develop a more tolerant and nonjudgmental attitude to life and to each other.

For empathy to develop, humans have to actually connect with each other. It is virtually impossible to truly empathize with someone through social media - such contacts are brief and usually superficial. Similarly, it is difficult to truly empathize with characters in movies or television shows because there is an insufficient duration of time and no real connectibility. People who spend most of their time interacting with others through media, do not have an adequate opportunity to develop their empathy skills. It might be easier to develop one's empathy skills by reading novels with deep character development and greater insight provided by their authors. Ideally, empathy should be developed through person to person contact in real-life situations to actually connect and "feel" the emotions of the other person. No wonder that humility and empathy are not thriving in the age of social media.

Empathy also improves communication with others. Listening actively and empathetically advances our understanding of others and the entire world around us. Unlike Kant and Hume, a person versed in humility is able to look for wisdom outside of himself or herself. One doesn't have to reason their way to wisdom, when all one has to do is open their eyes to the wisdom of others, especially the wisdom handed down throughout history. Although our technology has advanced dramatically, have human beings truly changed with time – or is human nature essentially the same as it was centuries ago? I would submit that human beings have not changed significantly from generation to generation: our humanness is essentially the same as that of our ancestors. We still have the innate ability to choose to do good or evil.

Humility can also predispose one to mindfulness. The modern practice of mindfulness is intended to allow one to observe one's own thoughts, emotions, and feelings in an honest and judgment free manner. The idea is to concentrate on the present, as opposed to obsessing over the past or worrying about the future. By doing so, one can recognize and control emotions and attitude. In a way, mindfulness is being gentle and kind with oneself, while improving self-awareness and self-understanding. It parallels what humility accomplishes by being gentle and kind with others, in order to better understand others.

THE DECLINE OF HUMILITY AND
THE DEATH OF WISDOM

Humility toward oneself and others allows us to become well-adjusted and kind individuals who are predisposed to generosity. It also strengthens other virtues such as patience, temperance, diligence, and honor. It also allows one to shift focus from self to others, taking pleasure from and celebrating the achievement of others.

All of these qualities are not only noble and good for society at large but are also beneficial to business success. Humility leads to a desire to be helpful, improving one's work ethic. Patience and kindness improve working relationships. Diligence and work ethic improve productivity. And humble people can make better leaders and supervisors. They restrain their own egos, and through empathy, better understand and encourage their subordinates. This, in turn, creates more commitment and collaboration. Humble leadership that guides rather than intimidates and expresses patience rather than imposing inflexible demands, creates an environment that motivates employees to innovate.

By understanding one's inner strengths and weaknesses, one can better focus on others and identify their talents and strengths. Strengths of others help compensate for our own weaknesses, just as our talents may complement someone else's needs. Even friendly competition is good as long as it brings out the best in everyone and it doesn't become all about winning. This concept will be explored further in the next chapter.

Humility's greatest gift is freedom. It liberates us from the desire to impress others. It frees us from the need to be "right" all the time. It suppresses the desire to get ahead at the expense of others. By acknowledging the limitations of our understanding, and being at peace with that realization, we continually look for wisdom through our life experiences. We understand that there is no "finish line" with humility. It is to be perpetually sought after and practiced. As a personal tool I have always liked the "Litany of Humility:"

> "O Jesus, meek and humble of heart,
> Hear me.
> From the desire of being esteemed,
> From the desire of being loved,
> From the desire of being extolled,
> From the desire of being honored,
> From the desire of being praised,
> From the desire of being preferred to others,
> From the desire of being consulted,
> From the desire of being approved,
> From the fear of being humiliated,
> From the fear of being despised,
> From the fear of suffering rebukes,
> From the fear of being calumniated,
> From the fear of being forgotten,
> From the fear of being ridiculed,
> From the fear of being wronged,
> From the fear of being suspected,
> Deliver me, O Jesus.
> That others may be loved more than I,
> That others may be esteemed more than I,
> That, in the opinion of the world, others may increase and I may decrease,
> That others may be chosen and I set aside,
> That others may be praised and I go unnoticed,
> That others may be preferred to me in everything,

THE DECLINE OF HUMILITY AND THE DEATH OF WISDOM

That others may become holier than I, provided that
I may become as holy as I should,
Jesus, grant me the grace to desire it."

Even without the obvious religious references, the prayer is a challenging exercise for pursuing humility. I can't help but wonder if the religious emphasis on humility may have been the reason that some western philosophers, such as Hume, discounted humility as a virtue. Ironically, by discounting religion, he discounted the virtue of humility and surrendered to arrogance. Conceivably, that is why he may have been unhappy in life and limited in his ability to reach true wisdom.

CHAPTER ELEVEN

EXPANDING WISDOM IN THE WESTERN WORLD

"To accuse others for one's own misfortunes is a sign of want of education. To accuse oneself shows that one's education has begun. To accuse neither oneself nor others shows that one's education is complete."
Epictetus

"It is the mark of an educated mind to be able to entertain a thought without accepting it."
Aristotle

"To be openminded is the greatest virtue."
Heraclitus

"Learn to be indifferent to what makes no difference."
Marcus Aurelius

"When we can stay close to the wisdom of our own knowing, seeking solutions to our problems in the sanctuary of the heart and not in the vanity of the

THE DECLINE OF HUMILITY AND THE DEATH OF WISDOM

mind, then we can pretty much trust in the unfolding mysterious wisdom of life."

Marianne Williamson

"The most certain sign of wisdom is cheerfulness."
Michael de Montaigne

"There are two things that one must get used to or one will find life unendurable: the damages of time and injustices of men."
Nicholas Chamfort

"If you don't like something, change it. If you can't change it, change your attitude.
Maya Angelou

"A bend in the road is not the end of the road… unless you fail to make the turn."
Helen Keller

"We find comfort among those who agree with us – growth among those who don't."
Frank Clark

"Some luck lies in not getting what you thought you wanted but in getting what you have, which once you have got it you may be smart enough to see it is what you would have wanted had you known."
Garrison Keillor

"It may be justly said that genuine morality is preserved only in the school of adversity, and a state of continuous prosperity may easily prove a quicksand to virtue."
Friederick Schiller

"Look not mournfully into the past, it comes not back again. Wisely improve the present, it is thine. Go forth to meet the shadowy future without fear and with a manly heart."
Henry Wadsworth Longfellow

"Do not dwell in the past, do not dream of the future, concentrate on the present moment."
Buddha

"Lessons in life will be repeated until they are learned."
Frank Sonnenberg

"We cannot solve our problems with the same level of thinking that created them."
Albert Einstein

"No man has all the wisdom in the world; everyone has some."
Edgar Watson Howe

"A pessimist sees the difficulty in every opportunity; an optimist sees the opportunity in every difficulty."
Winston Churchill

THE DECLINE OF HUMILITY AND
THE DEATH OF WISDOM

> "Knowledge is knowing that a tomato is a fruit. Wisdom is not putting it into a fruit salad."
>
> Miles Kington

Today, it seems everyone in the world is continuously speaking. We have talking heads on television, talk radio, and millions of people talking on cell phones incessantly. Even people on recreational walks can be heard talking into their headsets. It often seems as if everyone is speaking and no one is listening. In many ways, our conversations are like old-fashioned walkie-talkies: when you push the button to speak, you are unable to hear; when you release the button, you can hear but you cannot be heard. Today, popular culture has us pushing the "speak" button and never releasing it. The result is that we speak often but listen rarely.

Many are anxious to speak to convince others that they themselves are correct and aren't interested in feedback, let alone constructive criticism. In fact, many think that because they have a right to free speech, that they have a right to be heard or a right to force others to listen or even the right to be believed. Many believe that they have the right to shout, shout-down, and even bully those who do not agree with them. In many ways, it makes modern culture rude and uncivilized. As famed Peanuts creator and writer, Charles M. Schultz once wrote:

> "A wise old owl who sat on an oak. The more he saw, the less he spoke. The less he spoke, the more he heard. Why aren't we like that wise old bird?"

The root of wisdom is what we experience and perceive in the world around us. If we do not pause to listen and observe, wisdom is suppressed.

However, experience alone doesn't confer wisdom. It is just a necessary process, or component, which helps one along the road to wisdom. Repeated observations of multiple events allow one to discern how the world works, how people respond to stimuli, and how relationships develop. As one notices how events and actions of others affect one's own emotions, impulses, thoughts, and reactions, one gains insight as to how one interacts with the universe, and how one might impact others.

Fortunately, we are not limited to our own personal experiences. We can read books, learn history, study science and philosophy, and thereby gain insights of others, as well as learn the lessons of history. We can better compare our reactions to the reactions of others who endured similar situations or tribulations. We understand others by better understanding ourselves, and we better understand ourselves by trying to understand others who have endured comparable experiences.

Most importantly, if we take time to reflect, review, ponder, and accept inspiration, allow our minds to wonder, and practice mindfulness, meditate, and pray, we can learn from our thoughts, our dreams, and most poignantly, our mistakes, pains, and memories. The critical ingredients here are silence and time. Unfortunately, time and silence seem to be in short supply in the modern world.

Everyone seems to be in a hurry. Rushing to work, from work, to the store, to meetings, are all so common place.

THE DECLINE OF HUMILITY AND THE DEATH OF WISDOM

"There aren't enough hours in the day"; "life seems to be one giant rat race"; "I can hardly find time to think"; "I can't seem to be able to multi-task the way I used to"; "if only I could be in two places at one time". None of those phrases are unfamiliar to us. Everyone seems to be on a tight schedule – most of it of our own making.

Work schedules are a necessity, but many events are crammed into short periods of time with little rebound or reflection time in between. Our schedules aren't just on our office computers, but also on our smart phones and smart watches. They contain our work obligations, personal obligations, and family obligations. And of course, our children have their own school schedules, sports schedules, and structured activities – all of which require careful planning and coordination to get everyone to their respective events. Often, these events are spread all over town, and are sometimes scheduled at the same time. (And, of course, traffic conditions and road construction can bust even the best set of plans.)

As if the schedules aren't demanding enough, we have work emails, personal emails, texts, and social media which demand our time and attention as well. We check emails and texts during and between our meetings, phone calls, Zoom sessions, and formal work obligations. In the event we find time for lunch, we are probably multi-tasking then as well. Everyone seems to think that they can multitask very well, but research indicates otherwise. Despite our perception as to how efficient and productive we are when we do more than one thing at a time, studies show a dramatic decline in quantity and quality of work product when we multi-task.

The real results are stress, anxiety, and a sense that we struggle to just keep our head above water.

As we get caught up with this busy lifestyle, we lose perspective and disrupt our natural priorities. We tend to encounter each other tangentially, if not superficially. We lose patience as well as connectedness. We often sacrifice family life for work obligations. We are unable to find time to disconnect, reflect, think, and grow personally. How did our lives become so complicated? Who wrote these rules as to how one should succeed? Why does our popular culture demand more of the same to get ahead, "keep up with the Joneses," or help our children get a jump on everyone else's kids in order to get a good education, good job, et cetera. No wonder wisdom has been relegated to the back seat.

Even if we can carve out the time, how can we find "quiet"? Not only is our culture hectic, it is also loud. The streets are loud, traffic is loud, and motorcycles have mufflers which make them even louder than cars. Car radios are loud – some people aren't happy unless their bass speakers rattle your windows when they drive by. People have forgotten the lost art of whispering, and speak loudly in person (and sometimes even more loudly when talking on the phone). Other people's phone conversations are inflicted on you in restaurants, on streets, while waiting in lines, and even when sitting in doctors' waiting rooms. Lawn mowers, power trimmers, and leaf blowers drown out the sounds of birds and crickets. What does silence sound like?

We often have our radios and televisions on even when we aren't paying attention to them. Background or white noise is our substitute for silence. Even when it is relatively

THE DECLINE OF HUMILITY AND
THE DEATH OF WISDOM

quiet, we engage in video games on our phone or tablets, or scroll through social media platforms. It's almost as if we don't want to spend time with our own thoughts, or that we are afraid of what we might tell ourselves. No wonder heart disease, high blood pressure, stress, anxiety, and depression are at epidemic levels.

The pursuit of wisdom requires that we try to discover our place in the world, and where we fit in with our fellow human beings. We need to open ourselves up to new ways of thinking. We need to find harmony with each other and with our environment. Where do we start? What does it mean to be human? What is life all about? Is the old cliché correct: when we die, whoever has accumulated the most toys wins? Do we have a purpose? What is the true meaning of life?

I would suggest that it begins with another dose of humility. We are mortal beings – members of the animal kingdom. We share 99.9 percent of our DNA with every other human being, and the remaining .1 percent of our DNA makes us unique. We share 96 percent of our DNA with chimpanzees and 50 percent of our DNA with pumpkins. We are clearly part of this planet and are called to be in harmony with all of creation, including the other 7.8 billion human beings with whom we reside.

Besides sharing our DNA with the other 7.8 billion people, we also share mortality. From the moment of birth, we are destined to die. Despite our body's capacity to regenerate cells, we have a finite capacity to survive our environment and the pre-programmed life expectancy of our physical bodies. More importantly, we are apparently the only member of the animal kingdom to fully appreciate our own mortality. We learn at a very early age that people around us die, and that we, too, must eventually die as well.

The truly wise of every culture throughout history meditated upon the significance of death while trying to understand life. Death is the greatest promotor of humility. Our bodies predominantly borrow water and carbon from the earth during our lives and return them to the environment when we die – just as every other plant and animal does. The Ancient Greeks recognized this concept as "carpe diem", or seize the day – the brevity of life requires one to live in the moment and make the best of a short ride. The Romans coined "Tempus Fugit", or "time flies". The Romans also coined the phrase "Memento Mori" or "remember that you must die". By appreciating the brevity of life and the certainty of death, one appreciates the value of living one's life well.

The Jewish faith accepts death as a natural part of life and as part of God's plan. Judaism places a great value on life in general, as well as on each individual life. It encourages people to commit themselves to the paramount importance of preserving life. Christian tradition requires one to accept the inevitability of death in order to appreciate every day one is alive. In other words, by reminding ourselves of the inevitability and unpredictable nature of death, we are more likely to live in the moment with appropriate gratitude and zeal.

The Buddhist faith practices the Maranasati or meditation on death. Tibetan Buddhism practice Lojong – with four contemplations to cover a revelation in the mind – the second of which is the impermanence of the human body and the

THE DECLINE OF HUMILITY AND THE DEATH OF WISDOM

certainty of death. Although death is certain, the time and manner of one's death is uncertain and beyond one's control.

Islam encourages believers to ponder mortality and the vanity of life. Confucius acknowledged the certainty of death, and therefore, stressed living an ethical life with the goal of being sages and sharing goodness, benevolence, and love. Hinduism views a natural cycle of birth, life, death, and rebirth. The faithful stress the goal of good karma.

A dose of essential humility is a major step toward true wisdom. Wisdom places all of these concepts into proper perspective. We start with acknowledging our certainty of death (memento mori) as well as how quickly our limited amount of time will pass (tempus fugit). We can then refocus on the need to live in the moment (carpe diem). In other words, we can "seize the day" and make the best use of our time on earth - living in the present and being fully engaged in the world and with the people around us.

One should not be a slave to his or her past. Old memories should not control who one truly is or compel one to dwell on past pain or suffering. One should learn the lessons from the past, but not be defined by them. Instead, forgive others and forgive oneself, and then the past has no control.

Similarly, one should not worry about the future. Worry is a useless emotion. Rather, work in the present and maximize one's appreciation for whatever each day may bring. That doesn't mean that one should not plan for the future. Of course, one should anticipate future needs and set goals for the future. However, one should not be obsessed by what may go wrong, or what dangers there may be. One should never dread the future. Usually, when tomorrow comes, it's never as bad or as good as one might have imagined. Remember, if the absolute worst thing possible is death, and death is already accepted as inevitable, even death loses its power over you and you need not fear it.

Once the past and the future are placed in their appropriate places, one can fully concentrate on the present. One should open one's senses, one's mind, and one's heart to all that is good around everyone. Seeing the magnitude of the good in the world makes it easier to accept what may initially appear to be bad. Every moment is an opportunity to observe, to learn, to understand, and to appreciate. Take the time for introspection, reflection, contemplation, and inspiration.

Perhaps, most importantly, everyone has the opportunity to engage with other people. In addition to intelligent conversation and pleasant interaction, one can benefit from simply extending or receiving a smile, a wave, or a positive greeting. Even when someone is enduring what might be otherwise considered a bad moment or a bad day, a minor exchange of pleasantries can improve one's mood, one's outlook, and one's attitude. If, by chance, you encounter less pleasant behavior or treatment from others, let it slide off of you like rain off a freshly waxed car. You cannot control what other's do, but you can certainly control the effects of other's actions upon you.

This innate wisdom is available in all situations and through interactions with other people if one simply allows it to occur. It evolves from within oneself, as well as from interactions with others. Simply accept it freely, do not judge the source, and accept your own personal limitations just as you recognize and accept the limitations of others. After all,

THE DECLINE OF HUMILITY AND THE DEATH OF WISDOM

we are all imperfect beings, but we are not defined or held captive by those imperfections. We can recognize limitations, learn from those limitations, and attempt to improve and grow from them. This allows us to be open and authentic. Humility feeds wisdom, and wisdom reinforces humility.

Now, let us return briefly to the topic of death. Essentially, almost all world cultures and faiths stress the acknowledgement of the reality of death and the need to lead good lives in service to others. However, modern popular culture seems to ignore death, discourage morbid thought, and worship youth by striving to defy the aging process. Emphasis is placed on staying youthful in appearance and vibrant in physical being. The search for the proverbial fountain of youth has resumed, thereby humility is ignored, and wisdom is forfeited.

Pop culture is obsessed with child prodigies and the brilliance of the young. Today, many believe that the young are wiser than their elders – contrary to the tenets of almost every other world culture. Maybe this is because some parents, who never went to college, sacrifice to send their own children to college. After their children graduate, they defer to their "educated" offspring. Indeed, those students may be better educated and have more information at their disposal, but they are not necessarily wiser than their parents:

"I'm not young enough to know everything."
J.M. Barrie

"Good health is wasted on the young."
George Bernard Shaw

> "When I was a boy of 14, my father was so ignorant I could hardly have the old man around. But when I got to be 21, I was astonished at how much the old man had learned in seven years."
>
> Mark Twain

That is not to say that youth is not to be valued. Often children have the knack of seeing things that adults are blind to.

Children, as stated earlier, have inherent humility. They have an innocence, and sometimes say things that come to their mind without attempting to filter it. It may not be diplomatic, but it may well be true. The old adage speaks loudly: "out of the mouth of babes…" Sometimes the honesty is refreshing, if not painful, for the person receiving it. Many times, a child can express wise notions which might be considered "beyond their years". Nevertheless, just because a child may express something deemed to be wise, it does not mean that the child has reached a state of wisdom. What seems to be missing in that scenario is the level of experience and insight which comes with the aging process.

Wisdom is sometimes viewed as the sum-total of all that one has learned from living life – the total accumulation of knowledge and understanding. But wisdom also requires the ability to put it all into proper perspective. Those who experience tribulations and who have felt the pain of experience have the ability to learn from their scars. They can place the circumstances which led to the pain and anguish into proper perspective. As one gets better at putting all of life's experience into perspective, one develops appreciation and even gratitude for all the good and the bad.

THE DECLINE OF HUMILITY AND
THE DEATH OF WISDOM

That type of wisdom engenders empathy, compassion, kindness, forgiveness, gentleness, and genuine love for one another. One realizes that experiences are not necessarily unique to ourselves. More often than not, others currently feel the same emotions and pain that we do. It then hits home that we are not on this planet alone – there are literally billions of other people alive today who are in many ways more similar to us than dissimilar. Each of them has special dignity as a human being with the power of reason and the gift of free will.

Such insight provides us with the ultimate gift of wisdom – good judgment. Good judgment allows one to make informed and considered decisions and arrive at sensible and prudent conclusions. It allows us to discover truth – or perhaps it is better to say – to rediscover truth. Chances are the truth that we believe that we may have discovered has probably been discovered countless times throughout history. Unfortunately, those truths are not always well-received when passed along to future generations. After all, what does that old guy know about the world today?

Good judgment allows one to fairly judge another person's actions, but also explore the person's motives or intentions. In criminal law, most crimes have two elements: the bad act (actus reus – or "guilty act") and the bad state of mind (mens rea – or criminal intent). Generally, one can only be convicted if both elements are proven beyond a reasonable doubt. For example, when a pitcher in a baseball game accidentally hits a batter with a wild pitch, it would not be an assault because there would be no criminal (bad) intent accompanying the bad act of injuring another with a dangerous object (a 100+

mph fastball). In other words, the pitcher did not intend to harm the batter – despite the injury which may have been suffered.

The same concept applies in everyday interactions. Sometimes people say words that hurt someone else without any intention to cause that hurt. Countless family arguments start with words which are not well thought out; emotions erupt, verbal battles commence, and grudges are retained for long periods of time. These events occur among people who sincerely love each other, as well as among strangers. Wisdom helps one to understand the motives behind actions before responding. Or, at the very least, upon deeper reflection to understand the motives, stressors, and illnesses behind words that are hurtful and to provide better context so that the process of reconciliation can be commenced. That process of understanding fosters better understanding of and respect for others. Such wisdom lends to noble thoughts, noble actions, and altruism.

> "Let no man pull you so low as to hate him."
> Dr. Martin Luther King, Jr

> "No one can make you feel inferior without your consent."
> Eleanor Roosevelt

> "It is not that I'm so smart. But I stay with the questions much longer."
> Albert Einstein

THE DECLINE OF HUMILITY AND THE DEATH OF WISDOM

Mahatma Gandhi shared ten thoughts of wisdom that provide an excellent exercise in reflection and thought:

1. "Be the change." (Sincere change leads by example.)
2. "What you think you become." (Mastering one's thoughts allows one to master one's attitude.)
3. "Where there is love, there is life." (Love unites and strengthens us.)
4. "Learn as if you'll live forever." (When we cease learning, we start to die.)
5. "Your health is your real wealth." (We often take our health for granted until we lose it.)
6. "Have a sense of humor." (Humor is one of the greatest coping mechanisms and is linked to good health.)
7. "Your life is your message." (Are we leaving the world a better place? How well do we treat others?)
8. "Action expresses priorities." (Words are shallow – we tend to spend our limited resources of time, energy, and effort on those things that are truly important to us.)
9. "Our greatness is being able to remake ourselves." (Just as the earth regenerates itself every spring, we have the capacity to continually change ourselves for the better.)
10. "Find yourself in the service of others," (Serving others takes us out of ourselves – and allows us to help others while improving ourselves.)

CHAPTER TWELVE

ALTRUSIM

"Everybody can be great...because anybody can serve. You don't have to have a college degree to serve. You don't have to make your subject and verb agree to serve. You only need a heart full of grace. A soul generated by love."

Dr. Martin Luther King, Jr.

"Love only grows by sharing. You can only have more for yourself by giving it away to others."

Brian Tracy

"Never look down on anybody unless you're helping them up."

Jesse Jackson

"When you are able to shift your inner awareness to how you can serve others, and when you make this the central focus of your life, you will then be in a position to know true miracles in your progress toward prosperity."

Wayne W. Dyer

THE DECLINE OF HUMILITY AND THE DEATH OF WISDOM

"Remember, you're the one who can fill the world with sunshine."

Walt Disney

"We have so far to go to realize our human potential for compassion, altruism and love."

Jane Goodall

"Unhinge your ego, open your arms to love and let life's spirit flow through your heart."

Dr. Tony Beizace

"Loving others is the greatest gift we can give ourselves. Altruism that rewards oneself."

Alan Lokos

"Practice kindness all day to everybody and you will realize you're already in heaven now."

Jack Kerouac

"How selfish soever man may be supposed, there are evidently some principles in his nature, which interest him in the fortune of others, and render their happiness necessary to him, though he derives nothing from it, except the pleasure of seeing it."

Adam Smith

"The good which every man, who follows virtue, desires for himself he will also desire for other men."

Baruch Spinoza

"Few things, if anything, are more important than altruism."

Richie Norton

"Everybody wants to save the earth; nobody wants to help Mom with the dishes."

P.J. O'Rourke

With the realization that we are but a small part of humanity, and that we are a social species, we understand that we have a responsibility, if not a duty, to each other. We are not designed to be alone. We are by nature, interdependent, relying upon others for our very survival. Unlike other animals, our offspring are completely helpless for an extremely long period of time. Social interaction allows us to protect and nurture our young, support the weak, and advance our species. By social interaction, we have the advantage of gathering, storing, and preparing food. We have the luxury of developing tools to not only satisfy our immediate needs, but also to advance our society beyond just meeting necessities, to pursuing loftier and more noble goals.

Over time, mankind has advanced its knowledge and understanding of the world, developed the ingenuity to overcome dangers inherent in the physical world, and developed a much more complicated social structure. All of this depended upon humility and acknowledging mutual needs while coordinating diverse skills to satisfy the greater good. Empathy and kindness were a necessity. Mankind developed a team approach to everything including defense, hunting, foraging, and agriculture. Man learned to

THE DECLINE OF HUMILITY AND THE DEATH OF WISDOM

communicate effectively in order to advance the team's goals. Hence, all of these skills, which were based in humility and designed to advance knowledge, understanding, and wisdom are the normal and the natural state of humanity.

The actions involving uncontrolled ego, arrogance, conceit, and selfishness are not necessarily derived from human nature. Instead, they develop from unbridled competition for authority and power. It was fueled by a desire to accumulate material goods in an attempt to insulate oneself from future uncertainties such as drought and famine. Eventually, people tried to advance themselves at the expense of others. It was a deliberate move away from sympathy, compassion, altruism, and the comfort derived from being a member of a larger community.

Throughout history, that has been the conflict of humanity: those who seek power and dominance over others, versus those who seek harmony, peace, and tranquility. That conflict has torn apart families and communities, and has been the fire which ignites the conflagrations of war. Power versus weakness, superiority versus inferiority, and differences versus similarities, have divided humanity since history was first recorded.

As civilizations advanced, great philosophers would remind people of more noble concepts, as well as the benefits of wisdom. Arts and literature would prosper with the growth of philosophy, but eventually those civilizations would fall to more powerful forces who perceived wisdom, kindness, and compassion to be weaknesses. Throughout history, civilizations would develop, prosper, and eventually fall.

Today, people in the world are more connected and aware than ever before. Technology has advanced communication, education, and travel to unprecedented levels. Even language barriers have fallen to technology and computers which allow for virtual, instantaneous translation. Food, goods, and medical supplies move throughout the planet at rapid speeds and relatively minimal expense. There is massive accumulated wealth, and disparate world poverty. Despite the mechanisms for international cooperation being in place, altruistic endeavors often fail because of avarice and governmental corruption.

The world has more assets at its disposal than ever before imagined, yet there is no shortage of international tension and turmoil. The percentage of the world population operating under representative democracies continues to decline. Large segments of the world's population and natural resources are under the control of dictatorial and/or totalitarian regimes. The world is dominated by hate and distrust. Levels of anxiety continue to increase exponentially.

Hubris dominates humility; ambition dominates wisdom; desire for material wealth dominates noble ideals. Traditional values are mocked, kindness is viewed as weakness, and world religions are viewed as archaic and irrelevant. With the decline of religion, the values of humility, compassion, and altruism are further derided. Many who at least espouse virtue are often inclined to sell out if the pressure is too strong or the price is right.

Nevertheless, most human beings still value traditional virtues, even if their respective governments do not. Humans are naturally attracted to humility and kindness. People like

THE DECLINE OF HUMILITY AND
THE DEATH OF WISDOM

being appreciated and valued for who they are. They are naturally attracted to love, and desire respect and dignity as human beings. They appreciate freedom of thought, knowledge, and understanding. They have an unquenchable thirst for truth and the pursuit of happiness. They prefer to do good, rather than evil. They inherently love their families, communities, and friends.

That is why altruism is mankind's last, best hope. No one can change the world on their own, but they can affect change in the lives of those around them. If everyone would act kindly and generously to others, the positive benefits would naturally grow and spread.

As Dr. Martin Luther King, Jr., states in his famous "Drum Major Instinct" sermon, everyone has the desire to be the drum major and lead the parade. If that desire is for selfish motives, it can be a vice; however, if that desire is to love and serve others with a sense of humility, it can be the greatest of virtues. In other words, we should be drum majors for justice, peace, and righteousness. In so doing, we can make our current old world into a new and better world. Or as Gandhi said, we can renew the world by renewing ourselves.

It is not our individual responsibility to change the world on our own. We can only change ourselves and positively influence those around us. Because the task at hand looks formidable, one should not be discouraged. As American author, Jackson Burnett stated:

> "A thousand years from now nobody is going to know that you or I ever lived. The cynic is right, but lazy. He says 'You live, you die and nothing you do will ever make a difference.' But as long as I live, I'm

going to be like Beethoven and shake my fist at fate and try to do something for those who live here now, and who knows how far into the future that will go. If I accomplish nothing more than making my arm sore, at least I will be satisfied that I have lived."

If everyone were to accept that challenge, the world would be reborn and become almost unrecognizable from its current state.

So instead of trying to change the planet, concentrate on changing oneself. By changing your attitude and the way you treat others, you will become the sort of person that people will want to be around. People can change more readily by a good, sincere example than by all the lectures in the world. Positive person-to-person contact is the most powerful tool available to us. In the words of Nelson Mandela:

> "As I first said, the first thing is to be honest with yourself…you can never have an impact on society if you have not changed yourself…. Great peacemakers are all people of integrity, of honesty and humility."

This is further amplified by Pope Francis: "There is a danger that threatens… all of us. The danger is worldliness. It leads us to vanity, arrogance and pride."

People are naturally attracted to a sincere smile, a kind word, and acts of altruism. That interaction develops psychological benefits for all involved. The easiest way to make yourself happy is to focus on trying to make someone else happy. There is no downside to that activity. British writer, Steven Wentworth articulated ten steps to a happier

THE DECLINE OF HUMILITY AND
THE DEATH OF WISDOM

life: "1.) Be kind; 2.) Work hard; 3.) Stay humble; 4.) Be honest; 5.) Smile often; 6.) Stay loyal; 7.) Travel far; 8.) Keep learning; 9.) Be grateful; 10.) Love life."

Although happiness has many meanings to people, the common elements are harmony, contentment, and peace of mind. Harmony is reached through wisdom: understanding where one fits in with their environment and with other people. It is found by striking the balance between our talents and our deficiencies, our needs and the needs of others, and our desires and our responsibilities. Many are able to find that balance through religion. According to Radhanath Swami, author, guru, and Bhakti Yoga Practitioner:

> "Religion is meant to teach us true spiritual human character. It is meant for self-transformation. It is meant to transform anxiety into peace, arrogance into humility, envy into compassion, to awaken the pure soul in man and his love for the source, which is God."

That balance is also found in nature and in the inherent beauty and majesty of the world around us. As Confucius stated: "Everything has its beauty, but not everyone sees it." All natural and healthy ecosystems have balance. That balance ensures sustainability.

The second element is contentment. Contentment requires reasonable, attainable goals and appropriate effort in attaining them. The goals must be worth the effort required to attain them, and must reasonably satisfy a rational desire. And, of course, the goal must be attainable with appropriate regard for available resources and reasonable sacrifice:

> "Man, because he sacrifices his health in order to make money, then sacrifices his wealth to recuperate his health, and then is so anxious about the future that he does not enjoy the present: the result being that he does not live in the present or the future. He then lives as if he is never going to die, and then dies having never really lived."
>
> The Dalai Lama

By failing to strike the balance between reasonably attaining the goals, and recognizing available resources, one cannot reach contentment, and thus a happy life is also unattainable.

The ultimate benefit of happiness and contentment is peace – as in peace of mind. It is the ability to be at peace with yourself, with the world, and with others. But it begins with being at peace with oneself. For the world's oldest religion, Hinduism, Brahman is truth and reality which compels one to strive and reach dharma. The goal is a form of peace – to "help ever, never hurt."

According to Indian Yogi, Paramahansa Yogananda, self-realization is the knowing that we are one with the omnipresence of God in body, mind, and soul. Meditating on that realization can lead to tranquility and absence of anxiety.

Similarly, in the Buddhist faith, practitioners seek truth and nirvana, which is that ultimate truth. Among the eternal truths, is the middle way (a balance with not too much of anything) and the Eightfold Path to right meditation and a calm mind. Again, a calm mind without anxiety.

In Christianity, Christ greeted his disciples with "Peace be with you". Peace meaning not the absence of war, but rather peace of mind. As he stated in John 14:27:

THE DECLINE OF HUMILITY AND
THE DEATH OF WISDOM

> "Peace I leave with you; my peace I give you. I do not give to you as the world gives. Do not let your hearts be troubled and do not be afraid."

When you strike that balance in life, you don't have to be anxious or worried. Instead, you live in the present with an appreciation of the past, and a peaceful anticipation of the future. As the old adage goes: "today is simply yesterday's tomorrow."

When one has obtained the peace of nirvana, or the peace through dharma, or the peace granted by the God of Abraham, or simply the peace through modern "mindfulness", one can then share that peace with others. In the spirit of true altruism, peace must also be shared with each other.

One of my favorite altruistic prayers is entitled the "Saint Francis Prayer for Peace". Although it may be disturbing for some to learn that it was not actually written by Saint Francis of Assisi, and that it wasn't written referencing world peace as is often believed, it is still a great meditation on sharing peace of mind with humanity.

> "Lord, make me an instrument of your peace:
> where there is hatred, let me bring love;
> where there is offense, let me bring pardon;
> where there is discord, let me bring union;
> where there is error, let me bring truth;
> where there is doubt, let me bring faith;
> where there is despair, let me bring hope;
> where there is darkness, let me bring light;
> where there is sadness, let me bring joy.

Oh Master, let me not seek so much to be consoled
as to console;
to be understood as to understand,
to be loved as to love.
For it is in giving that one receives,
it is self-forgetting that one finds,
it is pardoning that one is pardoned,
and it is in dying that one is raised to eternal life."

Or in the words of the prophets of the God of Abraham:

"He showed you, oh, man, what is good; and now what the Lord requires of you but to do justice, and to love kindness, and to walk humbly with your God."
Micah 6:8

Altruism is the greatest gift. The more one gives, the more one receives. In other words, you may give of your time and your money to someone in need, but you receive a greater treasure in the joy of seeing someone else deriving happiness. What greater joy is there for a parent, than to sacrifice in order to see their children prosper? As Abraham Lincoln said: "When I do good, I feel good, when I do bad, I feel bad, and that's my religion." And in the words of John Glenn:

"If there's one thing I've learned in my years on this planet, it's that the happiest and most fulfilled people are those who devoted themselves to something bigger and more profound than merely their own self-interest."

CONCLUSION

"He that would live in peace and at ease must not speak all he knows or judge all he sees."
Benjamin Franklin

"I am not bound to win, but I am bound to be true. I am not bound to succeed, but I am bound to live by the light that I have. I must stand with anybody that stands right, and stand with him while he is right and part with him when he goes wrong."
Abraham Lincoln

"Yesterday I was clever, so I wanted to change the world. Today I am wise, so I am changing myself."
Rumi (Persian Poet; Islamic Scholar 1207-1273)

"Much of your pain is self-chosen."
Khalil Gibran

"All life demands struggle. Those who have everything given to them become lazy, selfish and insensitive to the real values of life. The very striving and hard work that we so constantly try to avoid is the major building block in the person we are today."

Pope Paul VI

"When we get too caught up in the business of the world, we lose connection with one another – and ourselves."

Jack Karnfield

"Two things define you. Your patience when you have nothing, and your attitude when you have everything."

Imam Ali

"Whoever undertakes to set himself up as a judge of truth and knowledge is shipwrecked by the laughter of the gods."

Edward Burke

"People who make up their minds about something never listen to advice – especially when it is to the contrary."

Steven Erikson

"It was pride that changed angles into devils; it is humility that makes men as angels."

Augustine of Hippo

" We come nearest to the great when we are great in humility."

Rabindranath Tagore

THE DECLINE OF HUMILITY AND THE DEATH OF WISDOM

"Life's most persistent and urgent questions is, 'what are you doing for others?'"
Dr. Martin Luther King Jr

"After all the cheers have died down and the stadium is empty, after the headlines have been written and after you are back in the quiet of your room and the championship ring has been placed on the dresser, and after all the pomp and fanfare has faded, the enduring thing that is left is the dedication to doing with our lives the very best we can to make the world a better place in which to live."
Vince Lombardi

At some point, a reader of this book will most likely ask himself/herself, "why are there so many quotations in it?" I can assure you that it is not by accident. The quotations not only reflect the clever insight of their respective authors, but they amplify the very premises and conclusions of this book. Most importantly, they demonstrate that humility, wisdom, and the interrelations of the two have been discussed since the beginning of recorded time and the planet. They cover insight from western traditions as well as eastern tradition, and all of the world's great faith traditions.

Attaining humility and wisdom are ongoing processes which never conclude until one gives up on them or stops living. They are timeless characteristics that have been pursued by humanity since organized thought began. We do not discover them and we don't really possess them; we merely borrow them in order to pass them on. Again as Abraham Lincoln once said: "Books serve to show a man that those original thoughts of his aren't very new at all." In other words, I might believe that I was inspired to write this book on this particular subject, but I must humbly admit that it is probably just a compilation of my life's experiences, my lifelong studies and readings, and all the words of wisdom spoken to me by countless family, friends, acquaintances, and perhaps, even foes. Regarding the subjects of humility and wisdom, there may no longer be any truly original thoughts but there has been a lot of thinking about them over the last several thousand years of recorded history.

The reader may also wonder if this book was written to advance a particular religion, or even religion in general. Although, I am not apologetic for my own personal faith and am happy to profess it, that is not the purpose of this book. The goal is to highlight two important virtues which have existed and were documented in many early cultures which predated all of our current religions and faith traditions. Those virtues, and all the secondary virtues and gifts which flow from them, clearly lend to civilized thought and conduct. As we observe a culture which is becoming increasingly uncivilized, rude, selfish, and often cruel, it appears to be a good time to revisit them.

Modern society seems to have an official aversion to God or any form of religious dogma. In a society absorbed with relativism, there is little time or patience for any clear-cut delineation between right and wrong. The result is a desire to not only diminish the role of religion, but to actively and directly attack it and to disregard it as irreverent superstition. Unfortunately, in society's haste to dispose of formal religion, it discards humility, wisdom, and most other virtues with it.

THE DECLINE OF HUMILITY AND THE DEATH OF WISDOM

Even if someone desires to disregard religion, or even any concept of a higher force, there is no need for that person to dispose of the very virtues which advance society and guarantee human dignity and mutual respect. By discarding virtue, the resulting vacuum has been filled with vice, and by discarding good, the void has been filled with evil. Similar to the yin and yang of ancient Chinese philosophy, the world is full of a natural balance of duality: dark/night; north/south; winter/summer; positive/negative.

Ironically, it may have been the strict dogma of established, dominant religions which drove many western philosophers away from God and precipitated a distaste for all religion. If one were an agnostic, that could be a logical position worthy of intellectual respect. An agnostic believes that one cannot know whether there is a God or not. The atheist believes (almost an act of faith) that there is no God. For many philosophers, atheism evolved into an anti-God frame of mind, which may have led the antipathy toward virtues associated with those individuals whose religions espouse a God.

The purpose of this book is not to debate whether there is a God and if so, identify a "correct" faith. The issue of faith is purely individual, and everyone has the right to believe as they choose. The objective of this book is to point out the advantages of humility and wisdom for humanity and society, regardless of anyone's spiritual beliefs. The reason for this approach lies in the need to embrace the ultimate gift of true wisdom: good judgment.

Once someone fully embraces humility and develops true wisdom (knowledge and understanding tempered by significant human life experience), prudent good judgment can be exercised. That judgment allows one to relate to and connect with others, keep one's power and authority in check, and eventually earn the respect of others.

My personal epiphany occurred when I was elected to the bench after thirty plus years of litigating as an attorney. Litigating cases on both sides of the aisle, in numerous areas of law, and across my home state and in federal court – including some federal cases outside the Commonwealth of Pennsylvania, I encountered many jurists of all levels of ability and temperament. As a litigator, I had to have significant self-confidence (sometimes bordering on arrogance) in order to instill confidence in my client, as well as to aggressively advance the merits of my client's case. When the time came to ascend to the bench, I knew I had to alter my approach to the law, and to life in general. From my trial experience, I had many great judges to model myself after, as well as a few examples of jurists who may not have been as humble or wise as perhaps they could and should have been. I knew the qualities I wanted to emulate as well as the qualities I wanted to avoid.

I made a commitment to exercise humility wherever and whenever I could. I promised myself that I would strive to treat everyone - litigants, criminal defendants, attorneys, witnesses, jurors or court staff - with complete respect and dignity. I also committed myself to making sure I gave the opportunity for everyone to be heard, and to make a sincere effort to understand them. I knew that those commitments would be hard to fulfill at all times. I just never appreciated how challenging it would be to patiently listen to someone

THE DECLINE OF HUMILITY AND THE DEATH OF WISDOM

who did not appear to make any sense, or to those individuals who didn't believe that they had to answer to any human authority.

There were those who behaved so badly and discourteously that the entire court proceeding was jeopardized, as well as those who suffered from such mental illness or labored under such intense hatred, which caused them to virtually self-destruct in court. Patience and temperament was often challenged, and the ability to understand was often impossible; however, I have yet to lose respect for the human dignity of everyone I encounter. Indeed, I have found humility to be my greatest ally and wisdom continues to be my clearest objective. Only then may I better discern truth from lies, and temper the sword of justice with the reigns of mercy.

But good judgment is not reserved for the courtroom. It applies in all of life. Parenting is almost impossible without the insight and inspiration derived from good judgment. Good judgment tempers angry words which could jeopardize friendships. Good judgment also restrains personal attacks which jeopardize civility and societal order.

Remember we are all equal in human dignity. Some may have talents that others lack, and others will have compassion to help others heal. We all have the capability to be humble, and we all have the capacity to cultivate wisdom. We are all born into this world and destined to die our way out of it. Only the timing and mechanism of death remain a mystery. Let us all strive to be our very best, to ourselves and to each other. And let us strive to strike a harmonious balance in life. In the words of Canadian lawyer turned author, Robin

Sharma: "Grateful yet ambitious. Worldly yet wise. Strong yet loving." And in the immortal words of Alexandre Dumas:

> "There is neither happiness nor misery in the world; there is only comparison of one state with another, nothing more. He who has felt the deepest grief… is best able to experience supreme happiness. We must have felt…what it is to die, Morrell, that we may appreciate the enjoyments of life. Live, and then be happy, beloved children of my heart, and never forget, that until the day God will deign to reveal the future to man, all human wisdom is contained in these two words, 'wait and hope.'"

EPILOGUE

In May, after writing the first draft of this book, and before submitting the manuscript for publication, I had the misfortune of losing my mother and stepfather during the COVID Pandemic. Although my mother, age 92, was in palliative care and had received her "Last Rites" prior to being infected by the virus, she was completely asymptomatic. My stepfather, 96, was taken to the hospital and successfully treated for the disease. Unfortunately, within three hours of his discharge, he died of cardiac arrest before he could be reunited with my mother. She passed ten days later at home in the care of Hospice Services.

That period of time was extremely humbling for me and my family. We were all extremely limited by our Governor's lockdown orders, and my parents' assisted living facility was in a lockdown of its own. In fact, we had not seen my parents for several weeks before we first learned of their possible infection. Their weekend caregiver called off sick Sunday (after spending six hours with them on Saturday). She reported all the classic symptoms of COVID-19 and submitted to testing. A couple days later, we learned that she had tested positive, and the likelihood of my parents coming down with the disease started to set in. Despite our prayers, my stepfather collapsed to the floor and was subsequently taken to the hospital. The following day one of their weekday caregivers fell ill as well. She tested positive as did my mother.

During this entire time, we would only have phone communication. We were unable to visit or provide personal comfort. We were completely helpless, and unable to have any impact on their circumstances. We simply had to wait in the hope of getting both of my parents back together in their assisted living apartment. Unfortunately, all our plans turned out to be futile. Even when my parents passed, funeral services could not be in our church and burial services were limited to ten people. We could not even console each other in the traditional manner.

It would be so easy to be angry and bitter. It would be so easy to blame others. However, humility allowed us to accept that everything was simply beyond our control. All of our communications with family were by phone, Facetime, and Zoom. We found ourselves more thankful for technology than we were angry at our loss of liberties.

We are, indeed, living in strange times. Although we all look forward to a return to normal, and perhaps even the opportunity to do a joint celebration of my parents' lives in Church, it may be a while before that can be accomplished. Unfortunately, it is unlikely that things will ever be exactly as they were before COVID-19. Lives and livelihoods have changed immeasurably.

I trust that life will still be good, and the world will be a wonderful place to live as we adapt to new changes and challenges. Hopefully, we will continue to be patient with ourselves and with others.

THE DECLINE OF HUMILITY AND THE DEATH OF WISDOM

"Therefore be at peace with God, whatever you conceive Him to be, and whatever your labors and aspirations, in the noisy confusion of life, keep peace with your soul."

(From Desiderata)

APPENDIX I

THE TWELVE STEPS OF ALCOHOLICS ANONYMOUS

1. We admitted we were powerless over alcohol—that our lives had become unmanageable.
2. Came to believe that a Power greater than ourselves could restore us to sanity.
3. Made a decision to turn our will and our lives over to the care of God *as we understood Him.*
4. Made a searching and fearless moral inventory of ourselves.
5. Admitted to God, to ourselves, and to another human being the exact nature of our wrongs.
6. Were entirely ready to have God remove all these defects of character.
7. Humbly asked Him to remove our shortcomings.
8. Made a list of all persons we had harmed, and became willing to make amends to them all.
9. Made direct amends to such people wherever possible, except when to do so would injure them or others.

10. Continued to take personal inventory and when we were wrong promptly admitted it.
11. Sought through prayer and meditation to improve our conscious contact with God, *as we understood Him*, praying only for knowledge of His will for us and the power to carry that out.
12. Having had a spiritual awakening as the result of these Steps, we tried to carry this message to alcoholics, and to practice these principles in all our affairs.

The Twelve Steps are reprinted with permission of Alcoholics Anonymous World Services, Inc. ("AAWS"). Permission to reprint the Twelve Steps does not mean that AAWS has reviewed or approved the contents of this publication, or that AAWS necessarily agrees with the views expressed herein. A.A. is a program of recovery from alcoholism only - use of the Twelve Steps in connection with programs and activities which are patterned after A.A., but which address other problems, or in any other non-A.A. context, does not imply otherwise.

Visit us on the web at www.aa.org

www.ingramcontent.com/pod-product-compliance
Lightning Source LLC
Chambersburg PA
CBHW072159100526
44589CB00015B/2289